Eph 6:10-20

Lucy,
thank you!

Harold K. Hu[...]

Rom 8:28

PRAISE FOR
From Basketball to Bow Ties: A Journey in Leadership, Self-Discovery, and Success through Service

"From Basketball to Bowties: A Journey in Leadership, Self-Discovery, and Success through Service, is an outstanding book. I found the book to be insightful, thought-provoking, and informative. The book challenged me to do some introspection and enabled me to learn a great deal about myself and my leadership style. I really enjoyed this book and highly recommend it."

—Kevin Sutton, founder of
Living Trophies Master Zoom Class,
speaker, and coach

"Direct, personal, and inspiring. Harold E. Harris Jr. writes with power, transparency, and grit. The courage to convert his most personal struggles into a set of leadership lessons that has guided his life is both captivating and thought-provoking. He is a force—an incredibly positive force—for leaders willing to take in his leadership wisdom, sit with it, and then decide to act to be all they can be. Anyone serious about taking their leadership to the next level will profit from this deeply moving offering. Open up to the amazing story of one man who has created a life of purpose—born out of talent, perseverance, sacrifice, and spiritual love—in service to the leadership potential of every life he touches. Share his journey to that place where you just know that you know that you know."

—Jean B. Gasen, PCC, PhD,
executive leadership coach,
information systems professor at
Virginia Commonwealth University (retired)

More Praise for *From Basketball to Bow Ties*

"I could hardly bring myself to put this book down without reading it from cover to cover. It is a must-read for aspiring and seasoned leaders. The book is artfully composed of creative storytelling intertwined with lessons that are easily remembered and applied. The author takes us through an inspirational journey of heartwrenching life experiences that have developed him into an authentic, transformational leader, passionate about every aspect of life, and compassionate as demonstrated by his selfless gifts to others, from learning to tie a bow tie to giving the gift of life."

—Shirley Gibson, DNP, MSHA, RN, FACHE,
Interim Vice President of Support Services
and Planning, VCU Health System

"'When the world speeds up, we slow down.' This is just one of the principles Harris examines in *From Basketball to Bow Ties* that any current or future leader will benefit from. Harris's ability to recognize experiences, people, and situations and translate them through the lens of a lifelong learner provides valuable insights that we can recognize and implement in our own leadership adventures. Sharing his experiences, Harris tells a contemplative story that will help many people throughout their journey of life and business. He is an authentic leader who has faced and conquered many internal and external challenges to make a positive impact on himself and those around him. Read this book and pass it along to other people as a gift to bring goodness to everyone as they navigate life and business."

—David Ingram, president of Capital TechSearch,
founder of Visual Workforce

FROM
BASKETBALL
TO BOW TIES

A JOURNEY *in* LEADERSHIP, SELF-DISCOVERY, *and* SUCCESS THROUGH SERVICE

Harold E. Harris Jr.

BELLE ISLE BOOKS

www.belleislebooks.com

ISBN: 978-1-953021-38-0
LCCN: 2021915603

Printed in the United States of America

Published by
Belle Isle Books (an imprint of Brandylane Publishers, Inc.)
5 S. 1st Street
Richmond, Virginia 23219

BELLE ISLE BOOKS
www.belleislebooks.com

belleislebooks.com | brandylanepublishers.com

Jesu Juva

When I thought you saw me, you not only protected that sacred place but stayed true to the boundaries of your soul. The crossings of our existence, led only by our love for one another, remains the greatest riches of all.

. . . .

To our children, Jasmine, Sydney, Elle (Gabrielle), Darius, consider this work of my loving truth a tribute to the greatness that is measured by your power to move our world forward through what each of you bring to it. I love you more than you will ever know.

To my wife and best friend, Cynthia Carol, our uniqueness in how we see the world not only makes us work, but it also makes us one. My last breath belongs to you, as my soul belongs to our Father in heaven. I love you.

To the strangers who will become friends of this humble servant, I thank you in advance. This work is dedicated to the one entangled within the myriad of the millions that my testimony seeks to find. I trust this work to reach you and touch your soul.

To the very few trusted friends of my youth, as well as those of my current and future seasons, this work only happened because of you and your wisdom, accountability, and encouragement. I cherish what we know without ever having to say a word about it. I am better because of you.

Foreword

Let me apologize to you right from the start. I can offend people easily. It is not my intent to do so, but I do. My directness is often misinterpreted for arrogance when in fact I'm only trying to not waste your time or mine. I get to it quickly. Let me own that right from the start. Some of you are going to be uneasy traveling these pages. Others are going to find it a humorous, inspirational, and thoughtful journey. There will be a few who quite frankly may not like the read at all. I remain hopeful that many of you are going to absolutely love it. To all of these and other possibilities, I say thank you. Thank you for choosing to take the time to explore something different. You could have chosen to be anywhere or do anything else at this moment. It is my sincere hope that something hidden within these pages stirs you to take new actions that move you closer to your dreams. That is the power of being open to the possibilities of life. There will be no judgment throughout our travels together, but I do have opinions, passionate opinions that hold no apologies. Sometimes you're not going to agree with me, and that is more than okay. In fact, it is within those differences that we have the potential to draw closer to each other through our varying points of view. What I look forward to is hearing from many of you about how your lens translates into focused thought that catapults you into your next adventure. What I also enjoy are the differences in how two or more people can see, smell, read the same thing—have the same experience—but extract vastly different meanings from it. That is my hope for you: that you somehow get exactly what you need from these words, and it propels you closer to your destiny and purpose. Open your heart, turn off the world, please put the phone down, and let us travel to a place that most of us find quite unfamiliar—your truth.

Again, thank you for spending your precious time with me throughout this intriguing escapade. Be well, stay safe, and let us grow—together.

—Harold E. Harris Jr.

"There can be no progress, no achievement without sacrifice, and a man's worldly successes will be in the measure that he sacrifices his confused animal thoughts, and fixes his mind on the development of his plans, and the strengthening of his resolution and self-reliance. And the higher he lifts his thoughts, the more manly, upright, and righteous he becomes, the greater will be his success, the more blessed and enduring will be his achievements."

James Allen, *As a Man Thinketh,*
Chapter 5: The Thought –
Factor in Achievement

Introduction

This journey begins with one solitary word placed after another. Writing can be therapeutic. Writing can be inspirational. Writing can sometimes be difficult. For me, what matters is that I begin. It only matters *that* I write. Now, for some, this may seem like a very antiquated process, but for me, writing is my preferred method of not getting in my own way through overthinking every step. Just begin exactly where you are. Don't get caught up in attempting to be perfect. There is a great quote that shared with me by a senior leader I often used to encourage team members and friends through situations that require structured thought: "Perfect is the enemy of good," Rich P. would say. I believe that. What is more important here, in this "now" moment, is that I also believe in you. This book is dedicated to you and the greatness that already rests within you. Please, do yourself a huge favor and never stop believing in the power of YOU. Who cares what *they* think about you? Other peoples' journey are exclusively their own. You are gifted, spectacular, and wonderfully made. You are unique and were placed here in this moment for a very particular reason. This book has been created to help you discover that very reason.

Embrace the power to start something new that frightens you, and don't ever look back. Your progress will begin looking and feeling extremely uncomfortable. It will be filled with stumbles, miscues, awkward moments, and immense frustration, but do not lose heart. When embarking on anything new, it is important to understand that before we can be exceptional, we must first be bad—mediocre at best. Perseverance, patience, and discipline will eventually reward us. As we transition through the portals of progress, we must first believe that success is possible. Remember, your story is already written. Here is what I mean by that statement: Whether you realize it or not, every single choice you make contributes to the ultimate direction of what we call your destiny—that outcome born from singular decisions made over a period of time culminating in an outcome we like, surrender to, reject, or deny. Every single day we have the ability to choose which destiny we will embrace; simple survival or an outrageously adventurous journey full of love, learning, family, and friends—the best that life has to offer. The bottom line is you get to create your story. So then decide to live the life of your dreams and get on with it.

These are the words that come to me, but they are not from me—they originate from a place well beyond my reach, from somewhere in the universe long before I was even a speck of a thought. A place full of endless possibilities from whence His greatness flows. A place most of us can only imagine. I am also speaking of The One whom created both you and me. Our glorious Lord and Savior, Jesus Christ. Can't you hear it? Do you believe it? If not, don't worry. You are not alone. Simple ramblings of scattered thoughts, you say? Let's just see about that. This story is also a journey of discovery in leadership. Not just leadership, but simple leadership lessons for us all that can be used to help you navigate your true calling through service to others. "Really?" you might ask. Yes, really. It's a thing. You really can achieve success through service by serving those you're entrusted to lead.

———

How do we learn the value of true, honest, effective leadership? Notice I didn't give you the buzzwords "transformational" or "transactional." There is nothing wrong with these terms when used in the proper context. If you are not familiar, that is okay too. There will be no judgements during our time together.

Is leadership taught? Is it found in the volumes of books written by well-respected literary savants who simply had thoughts and experiences which they either penned to paper or transmitted virtually that the world embraced as powerful, insightful, and true? Is it cultivated in the bowels of our individual experiences and then unleashed as a composite of lessons learned culminating in what we think we know leadership is supposed to look, feel, and act like?

The answers to these questions are a resounding, Yes . . . and, well, maybe. Yes, with some meaningful nuggets sprinkled with boundless optimism that allows us to yearn for what we truly want—that is, to be significant. To truly make a contribution—a meaningful contribution that impacts the lives of others through our own unique gifts. When it comes to our attempts to be relevant, especially in the eyes of others, maybe there should be more attention paid to our internal navigation than just to what someone external to our personal experience thinks. Could it also be a resounding no? Is that possible? Does it really matter? Is it meaningful that we all matter in this excessively compulsive world in which we live?

Yes. It really does matter.

These simple yet important leadership lessons are worth re-visiting because each of them creates a new paradigm that although in your current experiences are familiar may provide a new context by which you can elevate your thinking to create new outcomes. What makes these leadership lessons unique are that they belong to you *and not to anyone else.*

Because you are uniquely created for greatness (more on that later . . .), these lessons will have a significantly different meaning to you and your life experiences than it would to any other person reading these pages. Your trials, celebrated milestones, and challenges are parts of your testing that creates your testimony. *That* is why your individual journey with familiar themes is special—no one else on the face of the earth has *your story.* No one has *your unique experiences.* Therein lies the beauty of the adventure we may choose to share with others. That is why our individual talents matter. The extraction of a single concept, a solitary phrase or thought that has the ability to transform your thinking and approach to situations, will move you from a place of stagnant redundancy to meaningful introspection and action that will catapult your life into areas unknown and unexplored.

As you traverse these pages, you may be reminded of situations that trigger emotional responses in you. That is a good thing. Sometimes things we see, smell, hear, or touch may immediately trigger a memory. When those triggers are unpleasant, most of us may quickly dismiss it in a feeble attempt to move past it so we do not have to confront it. I say confront the trigger that creates an uncomfortable memory. Part of the growth process is learning to become comfortable with being uncomfortable. Whether or not the emotional responses are good or bad depends on what you, the reader, attach to them, so please be careful. Just because we believe something does not make it true. Let us enjoy this ride together as we discover more about not only who you are, but why you are here.

You are not alone. You have never been alone.

Book I
Basketball

Chapter One

For me, it all began when I was seven years old playing basketball in a cold military-looking barracks of a building and a man named appropriately, Bernie Mann. Bernie was a short but athletic white man who towered with a presence that spoke of confidence, passion, and a love for teaching others that was unmistakable. Although diminutive in stature at seven years old, in my mind's eye, he stood ten feet tall. I love him and his family. They consistently nurtured me and poured unconditional love into my life. Although I had a loving family who cared for me during my childhood years, Bernie and Dorothy Mann took me in as one of their own. From the moment I was introduced to their son, Steve, during our first-grade interaction at St. Patrick's Parochial School and all throughout our high school years, the Mann family's love for me was unwavering and constant. Their kindness was always genuine and pure. Some of my summers were spent running through their modest but loving home as well as swimming in their pool or playing in the garage with some gadget Steve was explaining to me—a boy from the hood and historic streets of Churchill in Richmond, VA—how to use. This family treated me like I belonged with them—not like I was separate from them. As I reflect throughout this journey, their love and discipline were nurturing parenting skills I will never forget and always be grateful for.

Bernie's passion for the game of basketball was contagious. He was also one hell of an athlete. Whether it was baseball, softball, or basketball, Bernie had the skill to play it. He was also very kind yet commanded respect without demanding it from you—you gladly gave it because of the character of the man who was unassumingly requesting it. Thoughtful and playful yet stern and clear with his instruction, he showed me what love looked like through the eyes of a man teaching a child's game. He was a titan to me, and I loved him and his entire family with all my heart. He was as significant a father figure to me in my formative years as anyone at the time of my introduction to a sport that would bring me joy and pain for decades to come.

Leadership Lesson One: The speaker does matter.

This fundamental leadership lesson we will explore on several levels. For the purposes of our time together, I encourage you to challenge the lessons that will be sprinkled throughout these pages because they are by no means exhaustive and all-encompassing. Again, they are unique in that they are exclusively for you and your life's journey to absorb. Your story, regardless of the stage it is in, can hopefully garner some benefits from this adventure in self-discovery, introspection, revelation, candid honesty, and most of all, positive action. To be and do better for not only yourself but for those around you, all framed by that sometimes-frightening word "truth"—not *our* truth but *the* truth. You know the one I am talking about. That truth deep in our core that we ultimately know is the gut-wrenching, when-no-one-else-is-with-us truth. The truth that pulls and tugs at us when we know we are not acting in our or others' collective best interests. When we deny ourselves the benefit of that reality, we cannot use it to nurture and create what we all want—to live our best life. We must not simply dream about what we could have, would have, or should have done—but do it. Live it. You are a queen. You are a king. You must believe it to already be true before you can even begin to see what is possible. Yes, you can.

When I first participated in an organized basketball practice, for the first time, I truly understood that who is speaking matters. In leadership, so much is won or lost during the very first encounter. It's paramount that during this crucial period, we as listeners or we as the speaker embrace the concept of service and not command. Command has the dangerous potential to move us into blind spots that have the ability to misrepresent everything we are about to say or do regardless of our authenticity or intent.

Command is alluring. Command is necessary. Command can be intoxicating. It is an illusion because it may not represent the complete reality of the moment. You as the leader may be completely in control and command a team of people, but do they follow you because they fear you or do they respect you as the leader and trust your direction based on your character that you consistently display? The illusion is in your flawed thinking if you believe that command is some all-encompassing reality that everyone else simply surrenders to. It is real on the most basic level because there are very real hierarchies that make up our lives—whether personally, professionally, or socially. Command is perception. It can also be unkind and self-serving. Improperly used, command has the power to destroy relationships, corrupt businesses, and fracture nations. Feel free at this moment to insert any activity (social media, music, politics, world affairs, sports, etc.) relevant to your experience here. Many people, some of whom we call leaders and some political public servants, for that matter, do not understand the true power they have at their disposal, the power *we* have entrusted to them through our implied or explicit vote of support. What is even more important is what we sometimes unintentionally give them through our apathy—the unrestricted license to operate with total absence of accountability for the collective good and not to just the privileged few. Some, however, come to grips with the awesome responsibility of what true leadership is. It is service to others and a purpose far greater than their own. What exactly do we mean by command? Do we mean power? Command of what? How is this important? Why should we care?

When Bernie spoke about the game of basketball, he spoke from a place of unbound love and unapologetic conviction. At the time, I did not know if what he was saying was true, but I did know that I flat-out believed him. Because I believed the messenger first and the message second. His delivery was powerful without being loud. He was assured in his knowledge without being pompous; passionate without being overbearing or condescending. Who is speaking matters for our leaders of today because if no one is buying into what you are selling, your journey becomes a lot more difficult. Bernie did not speak from a position of command authority, but as a humble servant purposed with sharing something so wonderful in the fundamentals of a children's game called basketball that we, as enthusiastic and raucous tikes, became transfixed on not only the messenger but also his message.

Take a quick look around at today's leaders. From politics

to athletics, to manufacturing, to international capitalism. Truly great companies, non-profits, and service organizations have one thing in common—the messenger. Whether you choose to call it personality, passion, style, delivery, or something else—people, companies, and small and large organizations are more attracted to the gift you possess and how that gifting is manifested. I was so fascinated with the way Bernie talked to us about basketball. He was patient, and he never seemed to hurry his delivery. He grasped the fundamentals he was pouring into us. More importantly, Bernie understood how to deliver his message to little kids. Learning that lesson about understanding who the audience is would come to me years later. I truly loved this man. He had my complete attention and full commitment to be the best basketball player I could be while enjoying the fun with other kids who were just as excited as I was. This game captivated me. Bernie was the ultimate salesman.

There is a myriad of fundamentals you have to master in basketball if you want to be considered even a decent player. Dribbling. Passing. Playing defense. Shooting. Not to mention the intuitive skills that truly great players possess, skills you cannot teach—how to read the flow and feel of the game. Having a "feel" for the game is intuitively understanding what should be done for the good of the team in the moment. It is understanding what play should be called for which player; realizing that a teammate is on a hot shooting streak and accepting that you should keep giving him the ball; knowing what play your coach is going to ask you to run long before he even gives the signal. Having this feel for the game is instinctive as well as improved through repeated experiences in the moment. The more you are involved in the game the more opportunities you have to develop this learned behavior. Some people call players with this intuition a "coach on the floor" or say they have a "high basketball IQ."

Whatever your descriptor, the dynamics of such a fluid game appealed to my youthful exuberance. After all, the goal of basketball is to score more points than your opponent and stop your opponent from scoring. Another fundamental is navigating both team and individual defense without fouling. How do we do that today? How do we lead, inspire, and motivate others without getting stale? Without losing our star players—our high achievers? Notice I did not say "everyone." Not "everyone" will buy into what you are selling, no matter who you are or what your gifts to the world are. Human nature lends itself to this interesting yet undeniable truth. You know it. There is always someone who simply refuses to be all-in and totally committed to the cause, no matter how just, righteous, or noble the leadership's vision may be. Naysayers will always have a seat at the table. Truth be told, they are a necessity. Naysayers validate our leadership journey, even when they do not even realize it. Without the naysayers, the doubters, the pessimists, and the haters, you could not get to your ultimate leadership destination. Reality check—your title is not the destination. The corner office is not the destination. All of the trials, disappointments, celebrations, and unexpected situations are the tests to your testimony that create and shape the leader you are to become. These situations are the actual conduit to your launching pad of change that moves your new destiny needle. The world of professional athletics, for example, is filled with spectacularly gifted human beings who understand that their ultimate destination is not becoming a professional athlete (although it could be argued that most of them believed that it was their calling at one time), but to use their massive platform to impact other people's lives through myriad non-profits or other social initiatives that strengthen us as a community—and ultimately humanity. I applaud athletes' selflessness to serve others through the platform their gifts provided and their hard work unleashed.

Great leaders need to be able to teach and inspire simultaneously without offending. It is an artful skill. Some possess it naturally, while others must develop it through practicing empathy. Even then, there are no guarantees. Remember that temptress called power? Careful: she can corrupt even the most humble and well-intentioned servant. They say that some people have the awareness to see its sultry allure, while others do not or simply cannot recognize what is slowly capturing their soul like the slow and deadly trap of quicksand. Can it be taught? Is it something that most great leaders are born with? Can you go to school for it? Can it be learned through experience, both good and bad?

Leadership comes from the ability to truly care for another human being on a level that supersedes commonplace expectations. True caring and compassion are inextricably linked. How do great leaders demonstrate compassion and without appearing soft? How do great leaders command attention and respect and without appearing domineering or arrogant?

Perhaps you are thinking, "Man, there are a lot of questions here." Well, you're right. And we are going to address them in great detail. These seemingly simple questions are complex not only in what they mean, but also in what they really convey when answered from a place of service and not servitude.

In the beginning, we established that the speaker does matter. True leadership has a vision. That vision is unrelenting and uncompromising. When Bernie was teaching that little seven-year-old kid from the rough Churchill streets of East Richmond, Virginia, about basketball, he did not mince words about the importance of fundamentals. He was crystal clear in his vision. He was compassionate and passionate in his delivery. But most of all, he truly cared about the message he was delivering and how it was being delivered. True, deliberate and thoughtful leadership matters. The messenger matters. The delivery of the message matters.

Pay attention to how the leadership fosters their vision, mission, and purpose. Be aware of their true motivations. Attempt to the best of your natural—and in some cases, supernatural—ability to discern why they do what they do. Is it to secure status? Is it for financial gain and power? Do they enjoy trying to fix and control all things in their immediate and not-so-immediate spheres of influence? Is it the adoration and compliments from others not as privileged with position and socio-economic standing as they are? Could it be the organizational mission and purpose to build something greater than oneself through others? We will explore the answers to all of these questions. Remember, the goal here is not to tell you what is right or wrong, true or untrue, but to stimulate your thinking based on your unique experiences, then apply the lessons learned to empower, inspire, and motivate your greatness. Your talents were not given to you for you, but for those around you whom you can choose to serve.

Mastering the basics is critical to basketball amateurs. This meant dribbling, passing, defense, shooting. In the leadership and business vernacular, this translates into understanding profit and loss (P&L), business concepts, emotional intelligence, strategy, poise, executive presence, timing, word choice, and delivery. Sometimes the absolute best word choice is . . . you guessed it: no words at all.

Confession time: word choice and delivery have taken me a really long time to develop. I have learned this one the hard way. Some would argue I am still learning. They would be absolutely correct. True growth—and not to mention leadership—is a continuous journey in learning, adaptability, honesty, and humility.

I was completely consumed with learning to dribble a basketball. In today's language, they call it having "ridiculous handles." I had ridiculous handles, even as a little kid. It was not because I was gifted. It was because I was uncompromising and ridiculously disciplined to practice the drills Bernie said we must practice in order to become decent basketball players. Remember, I was a seven-year-old kid, and the basketball was almost larger than me. That did not matter. Work needed to be done, and I had a vehicle: a child's game filled with lessons both real and imagined that I gratefully embraced at every opportunity.

Most people have heard the phrase "emotional intelligence" (EI). You may have also heard how different people define it. Some definitions may match your own; some may not. With respect to leadership, EI is the ability to quickly assess a situation and evaluate exactly what should be done in that moment, whether that be words spoken or actions taken. Truly inspiring leadership consistently understands what may be required in the moment for the good of the team or organization.

A key point here is that some moments are more important than others. Leaders who are devoid of understanding and serve only from the podium of position-power and reaction—they may have the title, but they are oblivious to the true needs of the position. They fear looking inept in the eyes of others due to the people-pleasing leadership character flaw and may consistently miss this fundamental truism. Whether you agree or disagree, I am asking that you consider a time when you needed solid leadership, and those in charge failed to meet your expectations. Did you recognize this failure immediately? You were likely disappointed. Disappointment is an anticipated and unmet expectation lurking just beyond the boundaries of what you believe to be true. You may have felt an unmistakable visceral reaction from this disappointment. Think about it for a minute. What you are remembering is the expectation that quality leadership would be displayed according to your expectation. As we continue to grow into more authentic and genuine leaders, it becomes increasingly more important that we let go of unmet expectations and embrace the reality that we all are supremely flawed human beings attempting to do what we believe to be appropriate in a given moment based on our cultural, physical, and emotional experiences. We will not always agree with those in positions of authority, but it is critical to our growth and development that we *respect the position of leadership*. When the foundational values of integrity, professional respect, and genuine love for the human condition are ethically consistent, morally familiar, and organizationally aligned, we have a good chance of making a real difference. When these values are not aligned, personal and professional organizational disruption may occur.

If our value system does not match that of our leadership, we may begin to acquiesce, rebel, quit, seek a compromise, or stand true to the misalignment between follower and so-called leader. Which do you choose? Only you can honestly answer that. I answer this question this way: "It all depends." I know; it sounds very much like a fence-straddling, play-it-safe response, but it's a smart strategy. Sometimes you simply cannot fight every battle in front of you. If you choose this ill-fated course of action, you may find yourself constantly on the outside looking into a moment that could perhaps have resolved itself without your interference in the first place. Sometimes we simply need to be still.

Every moment of clarity and decision may be matched with momentary uncertainty that will require a response. Some scenarios require compromise, while others require you to stand firm in your position no matter the cost. Other situations may require that you acquiesce and "live to fight another day." Choose your battles carefully. Still other situations call for you to simply walk away and disengage. We are not going to agree on everything here, and different people would make different decisions in potentially similar situations. This is what makes our journey together all the more interesting: discovery of what you know to be true for you and your experiences.

Emotionally intelligent leaders understand a situation and what is required in the moment. They know what to say or do that will inspire others to give more than they even thought possible, rally around a purpose or cause, or trust a new paradigm that encourages them to grow outside their comfort zone.

What does poor leadership look like to you? Do you recognize it immediately or does it reveal itself over a period of days, weeks, months, or years of consistent actions and decisions that does not put the interests of the organization first? Do you address it? How do you speak to it? Do you simply ignore it because some may say, "It's above your pay grade?" Are you willing to rattle the cage of your superiors when conflicting values and behaviors place you squarely in the crosshairs of right and wrong? It all depends.

Being able to manage myriad emotional decisions using ethical morals built on years of personal experiences provides context that can only be understood by the individual. Attempting to decipher a leaders' motives will not serve you well here. Intent can be better understood, but their motivations are of no concern to your journey, even if their actions impact your journey. Be prepared for this possibility. You have to come to grips with answering the question of how you survive and manage your own professional career horizontally and vertically simultaneously. You also must remember that you have a job to do, and it should not include having to burden yourself with trying to figure out how to best navigate actions of others that either stress you out or force you to not be your most authentic self. For those participating in these mental gymnastics *daily,* hats off to you. Whether you realize it or not, you are officially exhausted. We know the medical terminology, but we sometimes do not know how best to manage it: stress. Some people liken this practice of attempting to understand the inner, deep-seated drivers of another human being to playing politics in the office. On a certain level, I agree; however, managing the many layers of a morally conflicting circumstance begs another question: What is it worth to you? For those chasing the corner office or the next promotion, it may mean everything. For others simply looking to wield a greater level of perceived power, an ego-seeking power-play that satisfies the temporary chasm of insecurity may feel like the best course of action in that moment. Still others may only want to do what they believe is the right thing. We all have our intrinsic motivations. No judgements here—only observations and actions that require recognition of the moment, and decisive, unapologetic, and uncompromising resolve.

Your value system may not be properly aligned with those of people who occupy positions of authority that directly impact your sphere of influence, your position, and team outcomes. Other people's value systems have the potential to cause considerable disruptions in your leadership compass—your "true north," if you will. Emotionally intelligent leaders masterfully adjust what is required in the moment, but here is the important part: They *courageously* apply constructive, inspirational pressure that builds systemic cohesion to continue moving the people and the organization in the direction of their own vision.

Bernie understood this concept and applied it masterfully when getting a bunch of rowdy kids from St. Patrick's Parochial School in line during basketball practices. One of the things I remember about those early practices was that the long, barracks-type building was always cold! It drove me nuts. I hate cold weather. I hate being cold. I especially despise having cold hands and cold feet. It was terrible. I remember telling others, "I like basketball, but why do we have to play in the cold? We are inside! Doesn't this place have heat?" Bernie would calmly encourage me to refocus in the moment in order to reel me back into the fold. Another endearing trait I loved about Bernie was his kind admonishment—even when he had good reason to be a hard-ass. I love that man.

Again, Bernie's ability to explain concepts as well as demonstrate them when necessary was an example that stayed with me. What I discovered in those early days of basketball was that I had found something I was truly passionate about. Notwithstanding the cold, I fell in love with the game—and it loved me back in spades. Bernie instilled in me some ideologies in those early days that I will never be able to repay—love, direction, and purpose. The very game of basketball would teach me how to play it. It would teach me how to love it. The game would nestle me close and welcome my enthusiasm. It would fill me with a belief that I could accomplish anything if I focused, gave it my all, and gave it my time and energy. It promised proficiency of skill, rewards external and abundant, combined with an unbridled joy from doing something that, although it's fun to some, others found to be difficult, and yet sometimes no fun at all because of their physical limitations. Bernie would nurture in me a desire to experience the wonders of the game through the people, places, and experiences that helped shape my character development as a child.

Did you catch Simple Leadership Lesson Number Two?

Leadership Lesson Two: Truly great leadership has love, direction, and purpose.

What exactly does that mean? Great leaders love what they do. They have a direction they want to go in; they are purposeful in their actions and deliberate in their resolve. Their sense of direction is unmistakable. They do not deviate, nor are they distracted by exterior forces that are contrary to their direction and true purpose. They are unrelenting in their drive and determination to fail fast, learn the lesson, and continue moving forward. Remember: success is not only built in the wins. It is also built during the losses. Successful leaders fail often but simply don't linger in the loss very long.

Have you ever noticed how great leaders carry themselves? Pay attention to leaders you respect and admire. Watch them. Study their movements. Listen when they are speaking. When do they choose to defer? When do they choose to lead? When do they purposely relegate themselves to the outer periphery in order to grow others into their moments of confidence-building opportunities and self-expression? I believe you will find people who embrace the pressure of wearing the crown of responsibility. Leadership—truly great leadership—comes in all shapes, sizes, and colors. Great leaders are not simply relegated to the C-suite and corporate America. True leadership looks just like you. Getting you to believe this and then act upon that preordained destiny adds a note to the melody of your life. Trust it. Believe it to be already true. The only people who will be amazed by it are those who doubted you from the very beginning. There is a phrase used by athletes and coaches to describe the recommended way to handle winning: "Act like you've been here before." In other words, believe those things not yet seen as though they have already been created, and watch your world open up and embrace what others simply cannot see in you. Before you even begin transforming your circumstances, you must believe them to already exist well before they manifest themselves into the tangible reality of the world before you. What you believe in your heart is the catalyst that ignites the fire from within.

It may be even more important to pay attention to leaders you do not think very highly of. We have a ridiculously simple leadership lesson for that coming up as well. But for now, think about what "poor" leadership means to you—not only what it looks like, but also what it feels like. This self-reflection is critical to your success and continued growth. This exercise is for you and you alone. Remember, this journey is all about applying what you already have—the ability that somehow must be released. It's only available to those who believe it exists within them. Henry Ford famously said, "If you think you can or cannot, you're right."

Chapter Two

As we listened to Bernie coach us on the fundamentals of the game, we quickly learned that developing all these skills required repetition. We repeated many different drills for one purpose—to develop skills during practice so that when we played a real game, those skills would manifest themselves through muscle memory and conditioned instinct.

One of the fundamental drills I used to love was simply pounding a basketball from one hand to the other repeatedly, squeezing the ball with only my fingertips. Not allowing my palms to touch the ball combined with the squeezing motion accomplished several things:

First, it strengthened my little hands. On top of that, with the repeated pressing of my human hands against the composite leather ball, my skin began to feel natural against the ball, and the two surfaces almost stuck together. I'd come to learn as I got older that, with repeated handling, that leather basketball could almost magically secure itself as an extension of my person. The more I practiced, the more secure my ball-handling became. Although this may be hard to believe, someone with very small hands can palm a full-sized basketball with practice. Some of you may have heard someone with mad handles described as having "the ball on a string." You put it down (dribble), and it comes right back to you regardless of whether you toss it between your legs, throw it behind your back, or perform crossovers designed to put the defender "on skates" (off balance). Whatever the move, rest assured that it all began with repeated ball-handling drills.

That fingertip drill did something else for me. If you've ever seen a video of dribbling exercises to improve your handles, you will understand they all tell you to dribble with your fingertips. Fingertip control is so important because it is the last contact before the ball leaves your possession. It also strengthens the entire mid-section of the hand. The more fingertip control you develop, the greater control you have over how and at what speed the ball reaches its destination. Here's the short version: Better ball-handlers make better basketball decisions in real-time without thinking about them. Have you ever watched someone with poor ball-handling skills struggle to dribble a basketball? They look completely out of sorts. It is as if their bodies are not aligned with their minds, and the physical disconnect could be painful and quite hilarious to watch.

Even as a tyke, I practiced those drills over and over again until I could do them without looking ("Head up!" Bernie would say). Since I was a little dude growing up, it was unlikely that I would be anything other than a guard (specifically, a point guard). Bernie's persistent instruction that I keep my head up was because as a point guard, or "floor general," I had to be able to see the entire floor so we could run or execute the plays Coach Bernie was calling. I couldn't do that while staring at a bouncing basketball—hence the drills.

The final and most obvious reason for our team's dedication to ball-handling drills was this: good instruction resulting in physically correct repetition improves skill. Improved skill increases the holy grail for any athlete in any sport—confidence. Without it, even the best athletes are unabashedly exposed for the mere mortals they are. You've seen it. One minute, a popular professional golfer can look superhuman in all that he is doing on the largest stage imaginable—and then, the next minute, they look like a complete weekend hack unable to execute a simple chip shot. Or how about a professional basketball player who looks completely lost on what to do next in the final seconds of a championship-deciding game when his teammates need him the most? Confidence is as fragile or as strong as we believe it to be in the moment for which it is required. Merriam-Webster's dictionary defines *confidence* as: "a feeling or consciousness of one's powers or of reliance on one's circumstances." It is also defined as "faith or belief that one will act in a right, proper, or effective way." Confidence can sometimes be like a mist that vanishes without any warning to the unsuspecting kid trying to learn a new skill or the senior leader tasked with the responsibility to create an entirely new organizational culture uncertain about how to best move forward with developing new moments that synergize a team that's unsure of its purpose and direction.

As my skill and speed increased, so did my confidence. I loved to dribble, or what is now called by some "pounding the rock." While some of the other kids did not take dribbling seriously, it was crystal clear to everyone that I loved the game. If I wanted to stop on a dime, change directions, and then decide to do something unexpected or pass to another teammate, I could do it without losing control of the ball. I also noticed that not everyone had "mad handles"—some didn't even have decent handles, and some had absolutely no handles at all. Some of the kids fumbled the ball when it was thrown to them; others couldn't dribble if their lives depended on it. But some of the other children still found a way to at least work on some of the drills Bernie encouraged us to work on while having fun doing it. After all, basketball is a game. It should be fun. It should bring you joy. As a seven-year-old child, it was exhilarating to latch onto the very thing that spoke volumes to me by affirming that my time and energy was well spent in a place unbridled by the expectations of others. I simply loved to play the game, and no one could ever take that away from me. I could truly be just a kid in this space. There was a lot of fun in simply knowing that and living in it.

In effective leadership—or, as some leadership experts call it, "transformational leadership"—certain skills must be developed if you want to motivate others beyond what they believe possible. Let's talk about discernment for just a moment.

Discernment as defined by Merriam-Webster's as "the quality of being able to grasp and comprehend what is obscure: skill in discerning"—in other words, the ability to grasp clearly what may be difficult for others to see or understand. Effective leaders recognize opportunities for improvement well before others recognize that there is even a problem on the table.

Aside from the formal definition, the difference between EI and discernment is trusting what you cannot necessarily see but knowing and absolutely believing that it is present for those astute enough to not only feel it but respond appropriately to it. Learning to understand what discernment is and how it works is fascinating to me because up until a few years ago, I did not have a clue about what discernment truly was—nor was I emotionally or spiritually mature enough to receive it. That's right. No clue.

Nada. I couldn't discern a potato sack from a garbage truck.

Now, before I beat myself up too much about how to best use discernment, let me paint a picture for you. Imagine a friend or coworker says something totally inappropriate to another person in your shared social group—but the offender clearly has no clue they've just damaged a relationship. They are not even tuned-in enough to recognize the body language or facial expression on the face of the other person. Discernment says, "Wow! I can't believe they just said that!"

Wait just a minute. There are several decisions you must make in the moment. First, read the reaction and not the response. Next, verify the response from the offended party to better understand what is required in the moment—some action on your part, no action at all on your part, action on your part privately with the offender, or action on your part privately with the offended party. Discernment happens naturally through the unique lens of a sincere and mature perspective with an unselfish concern for others.

Not everyone has the same levels of discernment. Everyone has some level of common sense, but not everyone has the gift of discernment. But here's the good news: discernment is born out of the humility to receive the truth about self-reflection and improvement and then ask for what you truly cannot see to be made real and clear to you. Discernment is more than a feeling. It is a healthy, spirit-led conviction that leads you to respond and not react when situations require composition.

It is truly something you cannot put your finger on if you are unfamiliar. You simply cannot see it, figuratively or literally. Discernment is more about letting go than it is about being in control. You do not control discernment. Discernment guides you toward the light of truth—not *our* truth, but *the* truth. Sometimes those two truths are aligned, but when they are not, if at all possible, take a step back and through the lens of humility allow your heart to reveal what you may not see in your natural flesh. It may surprise you.

Leadership Lesson Three: Exceptional leadership systematically increases the collective "discretionary effort" of the entire organization they lead.

Before we begin, let us define "discretionary effort." We all have job descriptions that clearly articulate what is required of us in our individual positions. This serves as a baseline of expectations. Discretionary effort is additional energy expended that is beyond what is done in routine service for one's team, department, or organization.

Imagine, if you will, that Bob has been asked by Mary to complete a proposal with only the financial statements and nothing more. But Bob not only completes the proposal with the financial statements as requested, but he also adds the financial projections for the next five years *and* includes graphs with simulated projections! Some would call it going above and beyond. I call it positive discretionary effort. This effort inspires people to exceed their basic job descriptions because they are committed to the organization's betterment. Some people are intrinsically motivated and don't need others to instruct them on giving their absolute best. These people are simply wired to give their best. Discretionary effort is consistently exceeding the normal bounds of expectations that are derived from one's own formal duties as prescribed by the workplace. If this effort is not put forth, it does not negatively impact the person nor the organization; however, it does have potential to stifle the collective momentum of the entire organization if enough people become immersed in this quicksand of discontent, non-genuine left-handed praise peppered with quick-tempered decisions made without the benefit of all the facts.

If you want to quickly erode the collective discretionary effort of a team, department, or organization as a leader, here is a recipe:

- Add two (2) heaping tablespoons of speculation blended with unverified, anecdotal gossip devoid of factual evidence.

- Add three (3) cups of hyperbolic storytelling sprinkled with just enough truth to corner a leader into a position rife with blind spots (we will talk about those blind spots later).

- Mix four (4) servings of past misjudged situations that were discovered to be untrue, when you as a leader failed to apologize to your team for jumping to conclusions in the first place, which, if not addressed in real time, severely damages the trust-factor of the relationship of people, teams, organizations. Great leaders own their mistakes and apologize quickly for them.

- Add one (1) bar of reactionary behavior articulated via numerous email blasts packed with the arm-chair quarterbacking and exasperating barrages of emotionally irrelevant statements having nothing to do with the actual issue at hand.

- Bake at 400 degrees during multiple conference calls with extremely influential people, some of whom consistently display micro aggressive and passive aggressive behaviors as their cultural default.

- Serve criticism on multiple occasions, when instead of kudos you ask the judgmental "Why?" (A "why" question + criticism = judgment). Judgmental inquiries totally discount any good you may have brought to your team that they really needed from you at that critical leadership moment. People who ask "why" questions because they are truly seeking to understand a situation and gain clarity are perfectly acceptable. Leaders who ask "why" questions because they believe they have a superior answer or are questioning your *how*—not cool.

- When done, be sure to avoid accepting responsibility for failed outcomes that may have happened on your watch and take full credit for all successes that you had absolutely nothing to do with.

Repeat this process enough times, and there you have it. Before you know it, you will have folks eating out of the palms of your hands.

Of course, that's not true. In fact, quite the opposite. You will have successfully stifled, eroded, and contaminated any positive energy and motivation you as a so-called leader would hope to inspire in those in your care. The most well-respected leaders inspire, encourage, and move their team forward with optimism and belief that is much bigger than any one person. This is the leader we all aspire to be. This is the leader hoped for by those we are entrusted to serve. Challenge yourself to become that leader. There is no greater satisfaction than to have someone reveal that your guidance drove them to be and do better, not only in their professional life but also in their personal life. It is a goosebump-inducing moment that no status or amount of money can buy. It is real. It is forever.

Now, let's spend some time on negative discretionary effort. What does it look like in regard to leadership and management performance? The first dead giveaway is the word "negative." In this world of instant gratification, unreasonable and self-entitled leadership has been granted an imaginary high status that perhaps some of us "may achieve someday" if we work hard enough for it. I believe the word for that is "disingenuous."

Negative discretionary effort is the willful and intentional decision to purposefully give your very least in order to preserve energy and effort that is actually available for other activities. People work on those endeavors that are important to them, period. That is simply human nature. True leadership understands this foundational component. The ability to infuse what is important to the leader into another team member, group, or organization that reveals itself as overachievement does not disappoint—ever. One of the best measures of leadership effectiveness is how well the leader imparts their purpose into those charged with executing on their behalf. Likewise, creating an environment that drains the effort of team members to want to follow what is important to the leader is disappointing and exhausting for every single person involved.

Negative discretionary effort is created when leadership fails to recognize the sequence of events leading up to a critical moment when a team member, colleague, employee, or co-worker decides, "That's it. I'm done." This is the critical moment where you decide to check out and totally disengage—for good. Remember how we mentioned earlier that this decision is made willfully and intentionally? Both are true, but here's the rub: We are completely responsible for our decisions, and ultimately, we give control to others when we allow them to dictate our behavior. You've heard it before: "They made me so angry I just wanted to scream!" Well, that is simply not the reality of the situation. The truth is, "I gave them enough control that they could get me so angry I wanted to scream!"

Negative discretionary effort is a slow killer. It is a cunning disease that has no boundaries. It is not relegated to the worker bees only. It subdues organizations indiscriminate of a person's title, status, or position without warning. There are signs, but as I have mentioned previously, they are missed over and over and over again because we as leaders did not take the time to understand each other's role in perpetuating a problem you both had no idea ever existed in the first place. Marinate on that for a minute.

Take a moment and think about a situation when you finally "checked out." It may have been a conversation, an engagement with multiple people, or a one-on-one meeting. You remember it clearly, don't you? Here's the rhetorical question: Why do you remember it so vividly? Is it because you are hanging on to the pain of that situation? Is it because you have learned from the lesson that ultimately strengthened your character and built your personal and professional maturity? Here's the other question: Did you *stay* checked-out, or did you reengage in that particular encounter?

Before you answer that question, please give it some thought. Your immediate reaction to the question bypasses a critical self-observation that must be observed. "If I believe I have successfully reengaged and learned the lesson(s) of this particular situation, what does my new behavior look like? Have I demonstrated it consistently, or am I simply doing it temporarily because I'm trying to get something I need?"

We are inherently selfish beings who long for what we want more naturally out of self-preservation and immediate gratification than anything else. Addressing the true self can move even the most stubborn person into a sobering compliance that outweighs any lies they've told themselves to justify their behavior.

Let me be really clear here. Most people cannot and will not ever address their true selves unless forced to due to tragic circumstances like a disaster or another life-altering event. Finding your true self is that unscalable wall that is so high and so wide that you cannot climb over or go around it—you must go through. With the lies of fear in one hand and the sledgehammer of truth in the other, you must make a decision that will either fail you forever or propel you onward into your next and better iteration of yourself.

Decide.

Chapter Three

As my basketball skills began to improve, I discovered some interesting things about myself, which launched me into a journey that would shape my foundational belief system. I discovered that everyone is not equally talented or, for that matter, even interested in the things that I thought were important.

There were a couple of takeaways for me there. 1. It's not all about me. 2. Some folks are simply not good at what they may be doing at the time. 3. You are (or, in this case, I am) not skilled simply because you practice hard. 4. Remember: this is supposed to be fun! Learn to enjoy the game for what it is. It is, after all, not life or death.

I loved passing the ball and watching other people score! As I reflect now, based on what I've learned since then (I am a giver; one of my love languages is Acts of Service), it makes perfect sense now. Watching others succeed by scoring the basketball absolutely appealed to me. This was not because I was a point guard, a player who typically handles the basketball most of time, but because I had a positive, visceral reaction from witnessing the complete cycle of events unfold (the coaching play being called, and then the play being executed by every member of the team playing their role). To top it off, these things culminating in a positive outcome—it was like a field goal, to pull a reference from a different sport. Helping to create something successful that was much bigger than me was so special. It was exciting because it was all-inclusive. Everyone had an opportunity to participate—maybe not on every single play, but the concept of working as a team to accomplish something great became cemented to the essence of my core. I loved this game.

Being able to pass the ball effectively from one person to another (bounce pass, chest pass, lob pass, one-handed or two-handed) made the art of the assist one of the most enjoyable components the game for me. The ability to deliver your leadership vision can be mastered by learning multiple deliveries of the same message, which you can adapt for any given audience. Sometimes you need a soft bounce pass because you want to catch your teammate in their rhythm, so when they catch the ball, they have no adjustments to make. The same can be true of quality leaders who know when to deliver a kind and encouraging message, and when to press the team with a firmer delivery. Coach Bernie would call the play—a very specific set of instructions that directs the five team members to their assigned positions. Now, what if, after all of the screens and running around, at the end of the play I delivered a terrible pass that did not allow my teammate to be in the best position to score? Notice I did not simply say "to score." I said, "to be in the best position to score." There is a tremendous difference between the two. Ultimately, my teammate is responsible for scoring. That is part of the total team effort. Delivering a perfect pass does not guarantee success. Let's not even focus for the moment on the pass being delivered perfectly. A caring mentor and colleague named Rich once gave me some wise words: "'Perfect' is the enemy of 'good.'" There are times when a decent pass is all that is required. Sometimes, shots are simply missed. Passes are fumbled, dropped, or misdirected. Whatever the reason, ultimately the ownership for putting the ball into the basket rests with the receiver and not the deliverer.

Leadership Lesson Four: As a leader, you are going to miss the mark on some of your initiatives.

That is okay. What is not okay is ruminating on those misfires. The key here is courage. Courage is acting in the presence of fear. We all experience fear. It's what we do next that determines our destiny. Are we paralyzed by it, or are we invigorated with the very personal challenge to forge through it? No leader is immune to the fear of failure. Understanding and accepting that a mistake or miscalculation has been made and being able to move in a different direction for the good of the team—that is courageous leadership. There are lots of different ways to say it, but they all mean the exact same thing: move on!

Successful leaders have the ability to quickly step away from the internal demon that is trying to confound us all at times—our pride. It's almost cliché, really, when you think about it. Every biography about anyone of consequence is laden with examples of how they overcame some trauma or life-altering event that propelled them into the stratosphere of success, or fame.

Pride can blind you to the reality of a situation. Your lens can have severe smudges that represent your refusal to see truth due to what you think you know. Great leaders recognize when course correction is required. They set in motion a strategy that is not based on feelings but on data (P&L, performance KPIs, share price, margin, historical trending, market/industry disruptive events, etc.).

Back to basketball. If I spent time dwelling on one of my teammates fumbling a perfectly good bounce pass out of bounds and causing a turnover, I would not be able to perform the next action—getting back on defense to help my teammates stop the other team from scoring. Pride is deceptive. This cunning but dangerous character flaw can have you seeing things in a completely different context, blinding you to the reality of what a situation really is. Here's an example: I just hoodwinked you into not even considering the possibility that what I thought was a perfectly good bounce pass was actually, to the recipient, a terrible bounce pass with too much spin, which caused my teammate to fumble. Sometimes, what you think you see isn't actually what you see at all because you were not in the moment to fully experience it; you simply saw something and translated that into what you wanted it to be and not what it actually was. How about that?

What's the cost, and why should you care as a leader? Well, here's the good news. The mess you make could be remedied with some focused and very intentional effort. The bad news is that you may damage relationships, teams, or organizations by allowing your pride to run rampant.

At some point in our lives, we've all succumbed to the prideful demon. It can rear its ugly head at any time.

Having quality people around you who are not afraid to tell you the truth is so important. What exactly do we mean by "quality people"? Quality people will care about you enough to challenge your position, question a behavior, or provide counsel when you really need it—especially when you do not think you need it. Smart leaders have people they trust in their immediate sphere of influence. This crucial bond bridges the chasm of delicate instability that has the potential to keep most people quiet in order not to offend. Trust is critical. Trust is the thread that binds people into teams, departments, and organizations. Without it, people are simply individuals doing individual things, hoping it all comes together and sometimes not caring if it doesn't. Let's be clear: hope is *not* a strategy.

Remember: you've heard all this before, but it's worth repeating. Confident leaders surround themselves with people who are more talented than themselves. They enthusiastically search out people who consistently deliver positive results, stay focused in their swim lane (area of expertise), and stay dedicated to the mission of the organization—not only their particular department. Quality leaders want to be challenged, influenced, and strengthened by the collective good that comes from other people, regardless of professional station. Leaders not only understand the mission, they also clearly understand when their own leader is moving in a direction that is inconsistent with the organization's mission. By respectfully questioning a leader's perceived truth, a teammate or coworker can start a dialogue that, if open and honest, can galvanize a group seeking synergy.

Insecure leaders are dangerous. They will make decisions (or not make them) based on their feelings in the moment no matter the cost to the organization. They sometimes may operate from a deep-seated need to please others that has been perpetuated long before the evidence appears before our eyes in what seems to be a full-grown adult making adult decisions. What we see in the present is decades in the making, a series of actions that develops into the values that drive us to become leaders. There is very little room for insecurity and greatness to coexist. Weak leaders allow their insecurities to consistently overrule their business acumen. They place the temporary satisfaction of pleasing others over the greater good. This dangerous practice will eventually collide with unaddressed issues that could have been mitigated far earlier. You as the leader are driving the bus. When you see the traffic officer waving you in a different direction, don't ignore them just because the passengers were hungry, and the food sign said half a mile ahead.

Take a moment to pause and reflect on a time when you were certain that your immediate leadership was heading for a cliff. You could see the crash coming, but they refused to acknowledge what you had to say. Think about the situation not in terms of being right or wrong, but rather the best option for the collective good. Remember, this is not about me or you, but the organizational good. We often focus on the need to be right more than we focus on listening to and understanding the true context of what is actually happening that has led to this situation in the first place.

Which would you rather have? To be right or to speak truthfully to the moment? Well, you may be surprised that with either option, several outcomes are possible. The option to be right may be wrong for the situation. Alternatively, the option to be truthful is predicated on what *you* believe truth is. That may or may not be the case. Is your truth based on facts or emotions? Is it based on what you know or what you believe? Sometimes, no matter what you may think, it is simply not the truth, no matter how much you want it to be. Finally, it is possible that your choice may be inappropriate for the situation based on some or all of the information at your disposal.

Truth is defined as unconcealed reality. Water is wet, wheels are round, and healthy grass is green. Truth is directly in front of you and requires little to no interpretation by you or anyone else. We sometimes look away and pretend not to see it. I may not like the reality of what I see or hear, but it doesn't change the fact that it is still truth. Sometimes, getting to the truth can be difficult, especially if we have convinced ourselves that our belief system is right, no matter how flawed and illogically conceived the absolute correct position is. This self-absorption can lead even the best so-called leaders into an organizational death spiral if they are unwilling to consider that there may be a better way of doing things that has escaped their myopathy.

Being a leader is less about being out front than it is about people management, strategy, and execution. Great leaders don't seek out the spotlight; their deeds naturally attract the light that is required to accomplish the mission. That light guides the leader through what is sometimes a maze of uncertainty that gets reinforced along the way in a series of events that strengthen their resolve and trust of others in their care. As a leader, you naturally bring gifts and traits that make you unique. I call this "the core of your credibility." It means those things that validate why you are able to speak on matters to others and why they should listen to what you have to say. I must confess, this term is not mine. Jean G. and Ann D., two of my graduate school professors whom I adore and both mentors of all things leadership, brought this phrase to my attention. They both helped me understand that the core of your credibility is valued currency that is not to be squandered. What is your core of credibility? It is the expertise you possess that defines how you do what you do and your ultimate success. Your currency of expertise moves the needle when influence needs to be played individually or in tandem with another expert.

Let me give you a basketball example. Which coach has more credibility? The former legendary UCLA coach, or the guy coaching the YMCA recreation league of fourteen-year-olds? (For those not familiar with this basketball example, please instead compare to a star in your sport or activity of choice.)

Interesting. How many of you said, "Duh! Really, dude? UCLA! Coach Wooden!"? You would be correct in your assertion that Coach Wooden certainly has more basketball credibility with hundreds of college wins, NCAA championships, and a Basketball Hall of Fame career in his rearview, but would you be right in your assumption that Coach Wooden has more credibility? It depends of the level from which your credibility is viewed by others. Just suppose for a moment that the YMCA coach just happened to be your dad. Who potentially has more credibility now? You may still choose Coach Wooden, but let's be open to the possibility that your paradigm has just shifted a little because of a fresh perspective. That is my point. The more powerful a leader's core of credibility is, the more they must understand that everyone will view them from a different lens. It becomes increasingly important that leaders be in-tune enough (using their Emotional Intelligence) to be able to meet people where they are—not where *they* may be comfortable as leaders.

Your skill level simply gets you noticed. Your character moves the needle—the direction of which is completely up to you as the leader. The drivers that shape your character have the potential to be held hostage extensively or released quickly depending on how you as a leader (or, more importantly, as a person) manage your expert currency when helping others achieve their goals through the organizational mission. Nothing is more powerful than a committed team member who is serving others from the same organizational lens as those they are leading. Utilizing their core of credibility gives leaders good standing with others, which has value that far exceeds any amount of money. This is called respect. With it, leadership blossoms into a beautiful creation with a significant root system that will not be easily removed nor wither in the face of adversity. With growing and deliberate respect from the masses, true leadership will flourish by leveraging the talents of those who surround and support them.

Being able to utilize the core of your credibility to move people and teams has value well beyond normal organizational management practices. As a leader, you have been designated as an important "cog" in the machine that can either move the institution forward or stifle all momentum and create obstacles. Your currency is not to be squandered, but instead strategically utilized as a fertilizer for the soul, if you will—not your soul, but the souls of those you lead. Remember, they can see you.

What do I mean by "see" you? When you as a leader use your core of credibility for good, it manifests itself through unencumbered dialogue and meaningful insights that naturally align with the organization's mission. This dialogue is critical. It will directly impact every important decision you will make as a leader. Imagine that you couldn't be candid with those in your care, and they couldn't be candid with you. What are you building if not a relationship devoid of trust?

Trust is the crucible. It is the cement. It is bedrock. If you can trust your team to respectfully tell you the truth—even when it hurts—you can move mountains! When trust is built and increased over time, your influence expands far beyond what you may officially control, and folks accustomed to the status quo who may not want to move will do so if they believe they can trust you as a leader.

Now, let's be real and remember that some people won't follow you no matter what you say or do. That's just the way it is, so please keep it moving. Sometimes a seemingly simple change may not be simple at all to another person. Whether that change is a process, person, initiative, project, or institutional mandate, change requires a willingness to move differently.

It also requires a degree of faith that leaders understand may be hard to come by in the absence of information. To wear the mantle of leadership effectively, you must understand that you will not always have every piece of information at your disposal before having to make an important decision. That is okay. This is why it's important to surround yourself with others who collectively see far more together than you do alone. In this, your vision becomes exponentially clearer, and the odds of organizational success improve exponentially because of the focal clarity a larger, more powerful lens demands through shared participation and accountability.

Chapter Four

Let's talk about truth for a minute. Merriam-Webster's American Dictionary defines *truth* as "the body of real things, events, and facts." Truth used for good can be motivational. It can move an organization from a simple niche player to an industry leader virtually overnight. On the other hand, truth used to suppress, manipulate, or otherwise destroy (in legal circles, this is slander: false statements told with the intent to harm one's name, reputation, or both) is tragic and disappointing on many levels.

Level one: it destroys credibility. Level two: it destabilizes foundations through doubt. How do you build an organization on doubt? Level three: it can permanently damage key relationships that could otherwise be used to strengthen teams and entire organizations. Level four: truth used for personal gain at the expense of others rarely ends well.

Most smart leaders are uncompromising with this critical value system. They want whatever the details bring forth without modification. On the contrary, other leaders will say anything to manage, augment, or, in some cases, flat-out withhold information in order to protect others from any potential negative impacts of that truth. What is really happening is not them protecting others but quite the opposite—they are protecting themselves from the consequences not yet determined but firmly imagined. Operating out of fear is never a good leadership strategy. Your leadership decisions will not be universally liked by everyone. Rest assured that if everyone likes you as a leader, you are in serious trouble. This is vastly different from everyone respecting you. Poor leaders attempt to demand respect due to position. This unrealistic and temporary exercise in authority is guaranteed to lead to inconsistent organizational performance. The foundational component of fear is never a good brick with which to build a solid leadership foundation. We all know leaders we don't like personally but respect professionally regardless of where they rest in the organizational food chain. This truism speaks to the character of the leader, not the title they hold. You as a leader must come to grips with this fact if you are going to excel.

We've covered how truth is defined, but how do we as leaders cultivate an atmosphere of truth-telling that generates positive and meaningful momentum? This intentional behavior has the potential to increase the business bedrock—trust for our organization, department, or team. The short answer is that it begins with you. From the moment you walk into the room, human nature will lead others to subconsciously size up your integrity. We ask ourselves, "Can I trust this person?" We may ask ourselves countless other questions, so I will not presume to know what those questions are for each of you.

Let's remember that we've all asked, "Can I trust this person?" at some point in time. Sometimes, the answer may have come immediately. "Yes! I can trust them!" Or, oppositely, it may have been, "Nope. Under no circumstances am I to trust this person." Has anyone wondered why? Why don't you trust that leader to speak truth to you? Why do you believe they have your best interest at heart and can be trusted? Trust is built on consistently delivering outcomes that align with the organization's value system.

When a leader consistently demonstrates upright character by taking actions consistent with their values, when they are sensitive to the organizational need, truth has an opportunity to flourish. Some leaders simply don't want the truth unless it makes them or their superiors look good. They prefer to keep all bad news out of the direct line of sight. More importantly, if a leader participates in perpetuating the "frozen middle," if you will, there is a greater risk to the organizational momentum train derailing or grinding to a complete halt.

But why? Why is the fear of reality fraught with so much anxiety? Deep-seated fear and insecurity rule the day here. At its core, the inability to control the truth of what we may believe alters our ability to smoothly navigate the obstacles of leadership management. Great leaders embrace truth. They want it unfiltered and unencumbered by emotions and feelings. They want facts. They want details. Then, and only then, can they make the best-informed decisions about the future.

Great leaders instill a culture of truth-telling that permeates an organization and deposits itself on the front lines of where the rubber meets the road—the worker making the widgets, building the bridge, or answering the phone.

Storytelling is one of the most important "soft skills" a leader can have in their leadership lunchbox. The ability to give instruction through this medium can help create a lasting impression upon others that can exceed, for example, a thirty-minute PowerPoint presentation.

Great storytelling begins with better listening—more specifically, better active listening whereby we are truly tuned in to the words, thoughts, and actions of others in order to really understand what they are saying. By actively engaging in truly listening to understand the other person's perspective *before* we start preparing our response, we tune our channel to their station rather than our own. Masterful storytellers listen to the moment and then craft the most appropriate story into it just as easily as that once lost puzzle piece that seemed so elusive that now magically appears to fit exactly where it was supposed to. As we are all aware, hearing is vastly different from listening.

Throughout my initial introduction into the game of basketball during my formative years in parochial school, I learned to tell a story with survival at its core. I had nowhere else to go. I was alone. I was afraid. I was vulnerable. I was a child growing into a myriad of experiences well beyond my comprehension at the time. Creating a narrative in my own head kept me focused on what I loved most—the game of basketball. It provided stability during my youthful development that proved invaluable to my sanity.

It was 1980. "The Feast," as it was called, was pure hell. It was legendary. It was brutal. It was joyous. It was a crucible event. As a petulant freshman enrolled at Benedictine High School (now Benedictine College Preparatory Academy) located in Richmond, Virginia, during my freshman season, the stories of countless basketball hopefuls and their inability to survive the five consecutive grueling days of conditioning, basketball fundamental drills, and coaching humiliation peppered with total disregard for our physical or mental wellbeing are firmly embedded in my psyche.

Thirty or maybe fifty high school boys were confined in a small, hot, one hundred-year-old gym with no air conditioning and little ventilation. The appeal of this gym (called "the Barn") was not its simple aluminum bleachers one side and the green pull-out, old school bleachers on the left. No, it was the multitude of championship banners that lined the walls of this unassuming yet mystical location where some of the best from across the country would play. Another iconic characteristic of the barn was the steel rafters that charted the names of just about every cadet that has ever matriculated through this military educational institution. The names scrolled during the setup of the various military exhibitions or parties that were held in the barn when scaffolding was used to hang decorations. The cadets would use chalk in various colors to etch their names upon the forged steel beams and into Benedictine lore, typically with their year of graduation. Whenever I enter the barn, I've instinctively looked up to behold the tribute to yesteryear, the tribute to those who came well before me and a salute to those who would come after me. We were all vying for a spot on the junior varsity or varsity basketball team with the hopes of playing for Coach Rutledge— or, as we affectionately called him, "Coach Rut." Coach Rut was and remains one of the greatest high school basketball coaches in Virginia state history in addition to being a Benedictine basketball coaching legend.

Coach Bernie was one of the first and most influential men in my life that greatly affected my development. Although my family has been and continues to be a bedrock of unconditional love for me, Coach Rutledge and his assistant coach, Coach Hamner, reinforced in me the important life skill of perseverance that began to shape my character development long before I even understood what true character was.

Perseverance, or lack thereof, was quickly exposed in those who sought to endure "the Feast." Every year, this ritual kicked off basketball season and the subsequent tryouts. The months leading up to this incredibly difficult physical and psychological ordeal were exhausting. Although the details of the endless drills now elude my aging memory, as a kid just trying to survive, it felt like hundreds of full-court sprints and countless defensive stances. We endured chalkboard eraser speed drills, rebounding box out drills (which routinely resulted in busted lips, chipped teeth, black eyes, and bloodied lips), shooting drills, ball-handling drills, and running. We ran countless laps around that green and brown gym floor. Running, running, and more running. It pains me to think about it now, but I reminisce with a smile that speaks to four years of successful Feast completion. Other participants who chose to not endure the Feast and all of its agony must live with quitting forever. Even in the moment, all that damn running, I remember thinking, "If you quit now, you will have to live with that stench forever. It's okay if you get cut and fail to make the team, but dammit, you will not quit!" It's certainly better to look back on it now with a fond smile rather than a regretful memory filled with the woeful embarrassment of knowing I chose to not endure.

Cadets (Benedictine High School is a military college preparatory academy) began ruminating about the impending doom of the Feast months before the season. Typically, the chatter would begin around the start of football season. They talked amongst themselves sometimes or in other cases the seniors would enjoy inflicting emotional harm on some of the unsuspecting freshman like me by conjuring up stories of kids passing out from physical fatigue or puking their guts out or worse still—quitting. Giving up and stopping in the middle of the Feast was an irrevocable sin in the eyes of many. It was considered an act of cowardice, an act of betrayal to all those Cadets who, through the decades under the tutelage of Coach Rut, had endured the pain of conditioning on their way to double-digit Catholic State Championships. Even as a newly initiated dweeb like myself, one thing I knew for certain was that I would literally die on that basketball court before I would quit. My "why" at that time was far more significant than anything these coaches could do or say to me. No amount of criticism or ridicule would penetrate my armor. Even to this very day, few people would ever understand what drove me to survive those tests of the human spirit—both physical and emotional. How could they? Their walk was theirs to make, and my shoes could only be filled by survival fraught with love for a game that kept me safe when life seemed oh so difficult.

Chapter Five

Life is filled with seasons. One chapter ends, and a new chapter begins. The high school experience can be a daunting endeavor for most teenagers. Attending military high school adds a completely new layer of complexity. Let's not forget this was also an all-boy's academy. Sprinkle in the demands of military discipline, the rigors of repetition, seniors wreaking havoc on each freshman as a rite of passage into this academic and military fraternity—it was not a course easily traversed.

I did not handle the transition from St. Patrick's parochial school very well. In fact, I could not have handled it worse. As a scrawny, Afro-American kid from the rough streets of Churchill in Richmond, Virginia, I was not accustomed to hostile Caucasian dudes yelling at me, calling me names and making me do silly things—like run on top of the cafeteria tables at lunchtime, screaming at the top of my lungs that I was just a stupid freshman; or being rolled around the parking lot by other freshman like a small rug being prepped for storage or disposal while upperclassmen harassed me with obscenities; or doing endless sit-ups and push-ups with food being hurled at me. I guess, looking back, some of those times in retrospect are quite humorous, but at the time were completely degrading and far from enjoyable. What in the world was all that foolishness about? How was this hazing ritual beneficial for me in any way? What was the point?

Three things stand out. Obedience was the obvious first for me, followed closely by anger. The third, however, was far more opaque and elusive in its revelation—how to control my emotions and avoid being controlled by them. They were teaching me how to become submissive to authority and how to control my anger. Better still, they taught me what to do with my anger and how to redirect it to something more meaningful. You see, I was a very angry child growing up. Anger as we know it is a secondary emotion. It's a lens into something deeper. It tells us that there is something very wrong that must be addressed.

Leadership Lesson Five: Poise in the face of adversity is recognition that your amygdala is about to be hijacked and, if allowed to persist, the loss of reason and logic will be the consequences.

Psychologist Daniel Goleman first coined the phrase "amygdala hijack" in his 1995 book, *Emotional Intelligence: Why It Can Matter More Than IQ.* The amygdala is almond-shaped gray matter located in the anterior extremity of the temporal lobe. The temporal lobe is part of the limbic system, which controls anger and emotion. When hijacked or flooded with strong feelings, rational thoughts are significantly impaired due to the release of cortisol and adrenaline, which inhibits your ability to think clearly during this "fight or flight" period. Remember, you are being constantly watched by those you're entrusted to lead. Any slight deviation may be construed as something other than solid leadership. Attempting to always be in control is exhausting and can feel like a façade if left unaddressed. The goal is to be comfortable with our imperfections without allowing them to manage us. We are the gatekeepers of our emotions. They await our command. We are the captains of our ships.

During my long and tumultuous sessions with these testosterone-filled upperclassmen, I was repeatedly being hijacked, not understanding that the purpose of all of these interactions was to prepare me for something far more significant. As leaders, you must recognize when the "little monster" is about to rear its ugly little head, and you must cut it off immediately in order to maintain control of the moment. Maybe it is slowing your tone and speech; maybe it is listening as you battle the urge to react and speak over someone to quickly interject your thought; maybe it is smiling; or perhaps it is simply nodding in agreement and utilizing your unspoken body language cues to signal what it is that you cannot convey verbally because you know it is not going to come out the way it is intended.

As an adult, I can think of many emotions that may present as anger. Through many hours of therapy and revelations that would have escaped me if left to my own devices, I benefited from those around me that cared enough to counsel me—even when I knew I needed it but chose to marinate in the confused pain just a bit longer. The rest of my continued education was left to the maturity of others and the nurturing by those entrusted keep me safe throughout the journey.

Leadership Lesson Six: Unchecked and unresolved anger can ruin relationships and organizations.

As most of you are keenly aware, life can be the cruelest, most unrelenting teacher of all. Through these lessons, we must extract what is being attempted to be taught to us in the moment. All of us have moments where our anger gets the best of us. Leaders are not immune, nor do they get a pass. Regardless of the anger's origin, poised and effective leaders that possess the ability to recognize an infuriating moment and how they are physically and psychologically responding to it are like a bright, penetrating beacon from a distant lighthouse in the midst of a turbulent storm. People and teams will seek refuge in the steady and immovable island bedrock that is anger recognized but anger controlled.

Could my anger have been due to the death of my mother at the hands of my father when I was nine years old? To answer this question, let me describe how this event unfolded for me as a nine-year-old kid. It was a terrific summer day, and I was playing outside with my friends. Life could not have been better. My mom had gone to Washington, D.C. to see a play, and I was staying at the house of my mother's parents. Growing up, I spent a lot of time between grandparents' homes; my Granny, my father's mother, was my other summer destination. My maternal grandmother, Lila Mae, was also called Big Red because of her light skin color—and she was close to six feet tall. To me, she was Grandma, which helped me to distinguish her from Granny. My grandfather, Charlie Brown, Big Red's ride or die, was the man of the house. Although short in stature, he was a round, loveable man who used to kneel in his favorite chair at the window with his chin resting on his arms and watch us kids play in the street for hours on end with nothing but a joyous, quiet smile on his face, amused at the light-hearted, innocent exploits of youth at play.

Grandma beckoned for me to come inside in the midst of my fun with my friends. Jubilance quickly turned to indignation as

I huffed and puffed my way toward the house. My friends were making fun of me because Big Red was calling me to come inside. Looking back on that moment, what escaped me for years was the incredible poise she had while calling me to come inside. She was bracing herself to share with me news that no parent ever wants to hear, let alone have to turn around and share it with their grandson.

With a calm delivery, completely devoid of emotion, my grandmother said to me, "Your mom is dead." After giving me this news, she quietly left the room. That was it. No hug. No tears. No emotion. Nothing.

What happened next can only be described as unbridled rage. Me and my anger wreaked havoc on my grandmother's bedroom. I shattered mirrors, ripped clothes, destroyed furniture, and ruined anything else I could get my hands on. Just like that, my world was ripped to pieces. Was I angry that my grandmother had shown no emotion? Did she even care about her own daughter? How could she be so calm at a time like this? I now recognize the incredible strength it took for my grandmother, who was in that moment a grieving parent, to deliver tragedy to a child and then allow him the freedom to express it the only way he knew how.

To really understand how devasting this news was to me, you must also understand how truly remarkable my mother, Rosa Lee Brown Harris, was during her brief but exceptional time in this earthly existence. She was twenty-six years young on that fateful day in 1976. She was a beautiful, smart, well-educated Black woman, a member of the United States Army Reserves, and working on her master's degree from Virginia Union University. She was also a beloved member and faithful servant of the renowned Cedar Street Baptist Church that founded the Rosa B. Harris Women's Usher Board that bears her legacy to this very day. My mother was a gorgeous and fiery spirit that refused to simply accept a circumstance. She was not a status-quo, keep-quiet kind of person. Her nature was not confrontational but beautifully inquisitive mixed with an unbridled passion that few understood. My mom was a doer. She acted. She did not ask for permission, nor did she need forgiveness. It cost her her life.

During an intense fellowship moment (also known as an extremely heated exchange) with my father while he was driving his mistress's car, my mother demanded that he stop and let her out. She may have already been agitated that he had picked her up in a car belonging to his lover in the first place. My father never spoke about this detail years later during his recollection of that fateful day.

My father did not comply with my mom's demand. After repeatedly demanding he stop and let her out, my mother acted and did the unthinkable—she opened the door and jumped out of that moving car. Instinctively, my father slammed on the brakes and backed up to get her. That was the moment where it all changed forever. He crushed her with the very car—the other woman's car meant to retrieve her.

My father was charged with involuntary manslaughter and sent to prison. So began the bi-weekly journey to a place I loved to hate. It was a newsworthy local story that I remember seeing on Grandma and Charlie Brown's little black and white TV that was elevated by the Yellow Pages phone book sitting atop the little white cabinet in the kitchen. As I sat quietly against the cabinet doors below the TV with my knees held close to my chest, I probably appeared to be listening, but I was really in a daze while other family members and friends visited and discussed the tragedy playing out in real time for the world to see.

I share this moment with you as a reminder that behind every person and every leader is a story of glorious events and devastating moments filled with grief, joy, and pride. These stories morph into the very essence of the leader that person will eventually become. Sometimes there are more questions than answers. My father, in his recounting the events of that devastating day to me almost twenty years later, would draw me closer to his vulnerable humanity as a flawed person—just like the rest of us.

Could it have been from the consistent absence of my father during my formative years, or the side effects of his infidelity, insatiable womanizing, illicit activities, and overall piss-poor judgement to discern right from wrong? Could it have been from the biweekly visits to the former Virginia State Penitentiary with my beloved granny in her beautiful and sparkling white Buick Regal? (I loved that car.) For those unfamiliar with the Virginia State Penitentiary, simply picture the 1994 critically acclaimed movie *The Shawshank Redemption* with Academy Award winners Morgan Freeman and Tim Robbins. If I haven't watched this movie fifty times, I haven't seen it once. It is one of my all-time favorites. The purity of spirit and poise demonstrated by character Andy Dufresne (Tim Robbins) to endure in the midst of one obstacle after another is an inspiring testament to our human condition for survival. If you haven't already, do yourself a favor and watch this terrific, dramatic film. Your heart will be better for it.

The reason I mention this particular movie is so you can visualize the scenes that depicted the massively tall stone walls that were built to keep the inmates locked away from humanity. The state penitentiary was like that for me. Seeing those large walls as a young child, protruding from the ground and stretching to an apparently endless height, created in me a fear of finding myself incarcerated on the other side of those walls having to accept other people's terms via structured discipline. Not only was I angry; I was afraid of this place. I was angry that I had to be here in the first place, but I also was afraid of the wretched stench that infiltrated my clothing and every fiber of my very existence. The thought of never being able to lose all emotional attachment to that place was a frightening thought that I fought hard to eliminate from my young and very fragile psyche. Visiting every other weekend for years, I thought they would eventually do something about the awful smell, but they didn't—or perhaps they couldn't. More than anything else, I was afraid because of what this placed represented to me—complete failure to follow someone else's rules for your life. Rules that govern right from wrong; rules that say there are consequences for your actions, a familiar theme to which I was all too accustomed. I think that is why, even to this day, I don't mind being *asked*, even passionately, to do something. I will dig a trench with nothing more than a plastic spoon and willpower when someone says "please" and "thank you." Those two phrases fuel my movement and quickly indicate whether the requestor has enough respect for me to utter them. These words say that the other person cares enough about me to be kind first, no matter the ask. Now, keep in mind that going through the Benedictine gauntlet of repetition, structured discipline, and required accountability means that I have learned to have a healthy respect for positions of power. We can also recognize that sometimes when the boss says to go right, we must go right and execute. I simply don't like being *told* to do something—especially if it's an attempt to exert power through intimidation or position power. I own it. We all have our stuff; everyone is a perpetual work in progress. It is okay.

The unforgettable odors of fear, anger, frustration, sorrow, grief, and hopelessness—even as a young boy, this place disturbed my soul as well as my spirit. The soul of my inner being tried to make sense of it all during these visits to see my father, and the beautiful spirit of my mother, Rosa Lee Brown Harris, remained a part of me. Both were immensely troubled by this place meant to rehabilitate some and completely destroy others hellbent on never playing by the rules.

One thing I will always remember and respect about my granny was her unwavering spirit to endure. Her eternal optimism looked on the surface to be worry mixed with hardened resolve, which had been built through decades of self-sacrifice in service to others and enduring her two alcoholic husbands, whom she survived by several decades. She would pick me up and take me to that godforsaken place every other Sunday to see the man behind the glass window. A man I hardly knew. A man I would ultimately grow closer to but still never truly understand. He would die with a needle in his arm in the house of his mother, in an adjacent bedroom not twenty feet from her on a frigid early winter morning.

When I got the call, it was around 2:30 a.m., June of 1994. I was twenty-nine years old. Seeing the crowd of first responders, police officers, and medical and fire rescue vehicles with their lights flashing sent a chill through me. I don't remember how I got into the house or who permitted me to enter, but I will never forget what happened next. As I approached my father's bedroom door, which was slightly ajar, I could only see his arm hanging off the bed. A voice from deep within me said, "Do not open this door and see your father completely engulfed and defeated by the evils of this world. Do not give in to the desire to see what defeat through heroin overdose looks like. That image will remain with you forever. Do not open this door." My left hand, which was raised as if to open the door, suddenly pulled away. I stood there for what seemed like an eternity. I could hear nothing around me. The commotion of the fresh crime scene, detectives collecting evidence, police photographers' incessant flashing of their cameras, the "nosy neighbors" who had been awakened by the mounds of flashing blue and red lights illuminating the early morning darkness—it must have been chaos. I was oblivious to the details surrounding the chaos in which I was immersed.

The grief and trauma of what my granny had to endure on that day must have been heartbreaking. The noise of officials and relatives everywhere probably felt like a mob scene. I never heard any of it. In those moments when I stood near that bedroom door, my mind fell numb from the reality that there was no turning back. No rewind. No do-over. That moment, which felt like an eternity, was significant to my survival, and I somehow knew that. Not through any power of my own. Unresolved anger and fear can infiltrate and ultimately destroy when left to its own devices. My father was a good person who made poor choices. He was an angry man. Maybe he also feared becoming the man others believed he could become. And unbeknownst to me at the time, I was a very angry and fearful child, terrified of becoming a cautionary tale like my father.

During my exciting and turbulent years at Benedictine, one of the most well-placed people in my life was a guy named J. Romeo. Although the selection was a random drawing, it could not have been more appropriate. I called him Romeo, like *Romeo and Juliet,* even though his name was pronounced *Ro-MAY-oh*, because I thought it was cool. He humored me and smiled every time I addressed him that way. He knew my spirit and stubborn, purposeful defiance for authority was being removed from me with this hazing thing, so he cut me some slack by allowing me this small indulgence. I should have been addressing him as "Sir," as was the military imperative when in the presence of senior officers.

Romeo was my designated senior. All freshmen had a senior assigned to them during those days. He had sole responsibility for my well-being as a freshman. His job was to mentor me into a useful and productive cadet worthy of the corps. I am sure it was a daunting task for him, but he was exactly what I needed. He was my lighthouse.

Romeo was an accomplished guitarist with a huge, curly blond afro and a caring spirit. He was also as cool as cool could be. Nothing ever rattled him. He was smart as hell and well respected by the other seniors—at least in my eyes. He was the man. I can honestly say that Romeo was the best thing for me because he not only taught me how to handle hostile situations beyond my control, but he shaped my immature edges that forever poked me to a new reality—new situations are always going to require that you learn to adapt to what has changed and will continue to change. This world is uncompromising in its ability to swallow you up, spit you out, run you over, back up, and leave you for dead if you don't fight. I don't mean this only physically, but also emotionally, spiritually, and intellectually. My senior armed me with some of the necessary tools I would need to get through that first year and the rest of my life.

This is my story. This is my testimony.

I learned many valuable leadership and life lessons during my time with Coach Rut, who was considered a basketball icon and cigar-smoking legend. The military climate in and of itself is peppered with structural discipline that creates an environment which by itself is unimpressive. Collectively, however, it produces a whirlwind of power rooted by years of core values, hard work, unwavering beliefs, and systematic repetition. This was the Coach Rut way. Nothing mattered, not your basketball skill level, skin color, size, intellectual acuity, or desire to be a part of his teams. Coach Rut—and Coach Hamner, for that matter—were unwavering in how they demanded that basketball would be played.

The Feast poured the concrete foundation for greatness: the conditioning. You would not last—or, for that matter, outlast your future opponents—if you were not in shape. As a young, smart-mouthed kid from the streets, I found it ironic that these coaches who were supposedly athletic experts made us run endless sprints and other insanely difficult drills while they looked like they'd just left a Krispy Kreme franchise on their way to what we would today call a cigar bar. Remember, I was an angry kid.

One of my favorite drills during my four-year career as the

point guard on the basketball team was the three-man fast break against two defenders waiting at the other end of court. After we scored, or after they retrieved the rebound, the two defenders would take the ball and head to the other basket, while I, as the point guard, would have to sprint back and play defense against two oncoming, offensive players. In essence, three-on-two turned into two-on-one. I loved this drill because it aligned with my personality; it was me against the world, and the world was coming fast. The world didn't care that I was alone. It was intent on running me over if I didn't defend myself. On multiple occasions, the second my opposing teammates got the ball and headed in the other direction, I would smile as if to say, "Bring it! I'm going to stop you both from scoring *and* get the ball back!" It was personal. Coach Rut loved the scrappy, undersized kids who simply outworked the more naturally talented players through excessive repetition and relentless attention to details that more gifted players chose to ignore. I was not a super-gifted basketball player, but I had ridiculous handles. I was a better than average shooter—not a great shooter by any means, and I was blessed with serious "hops." I could dunk a basketball, believe it or not, because I spent so much time in the weight room working on my leg strength. I just outworked those who were more skillful and simply better players than I was. I eventually surpassed some of those players with my improved skill while others were simply more gifted and more talented.

When those two players came at me hard with the intention of scoring, I danced and jerked at one oncoming player to force him to give up the ball while pulling at his jersey so he couldn't move. This gave me time to get to the other player, who was heading to the basket intent on receiving the pass that his teammate had already made. By the time I got to the player attempting to score, they were either going to attempt a lay-up or short jump shot. My goal? No lay-ups. I preferred to make them attempt a shot as far away from the basket as possible. My odds improved the further I could keep them from the basket. Then, I would race to get the rebound and only worry about the one player I had to box out in order to secure the rebound.

I have thus far failed to mention that I did not always play fair. I guess I had learned through my life experiences that because life wasn't always going to be fair, I didn't have to always play fair —I could bend the rules without breaking them. I wanted to stretch the bounds of what was acceptable and do all I could to win. This doesn't mean I was willing to hurt others along the way. Great leaders don't leave in their wake a bunch of disgruntled and weary professionals just to accomplish their mission. There will be however some collateral damage that may result from some of the decisions required to move the organization forward to better.

It was during these rebounding battles that I cheated the most. I was already undersized, so I grabbed, pushed, and fought with everything I had to secure that rebound and achieve my goal: stopping them from scoring and getting the ball back. The world was not going to take from me without a fight! This was my ball. This was my life. Another player would not be allowed to simply have their way with me as a spectator in a drill. I am not the kind of person to allow you to push me around. Every play was a battle, and I was determined to win. The failure is not in the attempt missed; the failure is making no attempt at all. The failure is sitting on the sideline—watching life happen to you without responding in some way. To paint my personality as naturally combative would be taking the easy road, and it does not accurately depict the truth. Fighters fight not because they need the confrontation, but because the confrontation is already there, and it needs to be addressed.

Success came more often than defeat during these epic battles with guys who wanted to win just as much as I did. Sometimes I wound up on the worse end of the stick. That looked like a black eye, a busted lip, scratches, or worse still, the defeat of being scored upon. That hurt worse than any injury. That was my ego taking a beating. Those and countless other basketball drills not only increased proficiency through repetition; they also developed character through a sport that some can relate to. For others, it may have been baseball, cheerleading, tennis, or another sport. For me, it was basketball. I loved this game. This game loved me back.

Chapter Six

Have you ever wondered why some leaders succumb to the illusion that being liked by the people they lead somehow removes the responsibility of serving as a genuine steward to the position? This may feel like an abrupt segue, but it bears discussion.

Is it more important to be liked than it is to lead successfully? Rhetorical, I know. But perhaps we must define "success" before we address the original question. Whose success are we talking about? The leader or those who follow the leader? Both or neither? How can a leader inspire meaningful, personal, intrinsically motivated self-awareness in those they lead that it leaves an unresolved void that produces the desires we all aspire to achieve? We go through these mental gymnastics routinely without even realizing it.

Try to imagine having to decide matters of critical business strategy, make important family decisions, or evaluate life-defining choices primarily through the lens of fear. The need to be liked and acknowledged by others is not detrimental in and of itself. We all want that, and we all need others who come from healthy relationship building. This is the human experience lived well.

The unhealthy, self-defeating language and accompanying mental dialogue is rooted in a lack of self-acceptance, a failure to understand how truly powerful we are. The world as we know it inundates us with constant commercials, documentaries, movies and—you guessed it—books about how woefully insufficient we are. To no one's surprise, here comes the *next* panacea that will solve whatever ails our malnourished souls. My intent here is to get you to understand how magnificent you already are! The world will have you believe you're confused; you don't know what is best in your life, and you need other people's products and promotions in order to be made whole. You don't need to hear how unworthy you are. What we all need from time to time is a little encouragement, guidance, a fresh perspective, and a plan that moves us forward but is not predicated on the advancement of someone else. You don't have to lose for others to win. We are sometimes easily tricked into believing the worst about ourselves, so we self-medicate with our drug of choice—overeating, shopping, drinking, obsessing over social media, isolating, or making poor decisions that anesthetize the pain of our perceived inadequacy.

Leadership Lesson Seven: Not everyone is going to like you or the leadership decisions you make.

Heavy is the head that wears the crown, but you must embrace this truism in order to move past mediocrity—the stagnation of status quo. Better, richer, more meaningful outcomes await us.

The old adage goes something like this: "If everyone likes you, rest assured you are doing something wrong." Being well thought of because of your specific skill set, ability to consistently deliver positive outcomes, and kindness are vastly different than being well regarded for as a slithering corporate carpetbagger seeking to mask a multitude of personal and professional deficiencies. The mask consists of numerous moves made by fraternizing, cajoling, and otherwise not-so-subtle check-ins to gauge the level of non-transparency required in order to maintain a set of illusions that mimic genuine leadership and competence. Don't get this twisted. Being a leader who is responsible for the well-being of other professionals—not simply being in charge—is hard even on your best day. It is demanding. It is genuine. It is rewarding. It is sincere. It is servant. The difference between being a leader and being in charge is that people who are merely in charge deliberately express their authority as a way of signaling to others that all roads lead back to them. They are not serving others. They are serving themselves through the egocentric lens of their own personal gratifications that are stained with deep-seated, unmasked insecurities. They are just telling people what to do because it makes them feel in control. Leaders are willingly followed and believed in by others when they consistently exercise the servant mindset rooted in humility, not arrogance. The followers are galvanized by the leader's competence, compassion, and vision that is demonstrated by how they serve the very people that have chosen to follow them.

How do you typically react when your decisions create hope, optimism, stability, tension, angst, or fear? Do you over-explain without proper context, which in and of itself creates even more confusion and anxiety, or do you teeter to the other side of good intentions and choose not to communicate at all, hoping those around you will somehow discern your message and process accordingly? This is wishful thinking at best and total denial at worse. Get that sand off you collar and get on with it. You already know the word. I don't even have to say it.

The leaders who inspire you work on their craft of communication. They learn to deliver the message in terms that build not destroy. Some very wise leaders emphatically agree that the manner in which a message is delivered is directly related to how others may receive or reject it. Statistical research aside, we already know through our own experiences that some people are "blessed" with the innate ability to quickly and easily offend others in how they deliver a message. Guilty as charged.

Before moving on, it is confession time. I'm smiling as I write this. My passion sometimes gets the best of me. I have made considerable progress in the attempts to have complete mastery of this trait, and I can honestly say that I am better today than I was last week, last month, or even last year. I'm not grinning, believing that I do not offend. I smile because I remember people who I have a great deal of love and respect for—my lovely wife, Cynthia; my children, Jasmine, Sydney, Gabby, and Darius; and my cousin Michelle. And then there is my cousin who is more like a big sister, Denise, who since we were children has been "in charge" of me and never lets me forget it; other family members; mentors and professional colleagues. As I recall they all say the same thing, "Dude, your delivery could use some work. Less vinegar and just a tad bit more honey will go a lot further." I own it. I do not run away from it. I actually embrace stripping away the minutia of crucial conversations and getting to the meat. Now, before your little voice in your head says, "Well, Harold, you can get your point across without pissing people off in the process." I would say that you are completely correct, and I agree with you. I continue to be a work in progress, and I remain grateful to those who care enough about my well-being to hold me accountable for my actions. Every leader should have a trusted group of people who from time to time remind them that they do not walk on water.

Here's what I would like for every reader to consider in their personal journey of leadership wellness and self-discovery. Passion and the potential uncomfortable conversations that it may bring from time to time can be a slippery slope that requires all of us to be openly vulnerable for a minute. As leaders moving organizations forward, for us to even begin to see the wellspring of open dialogue and organizational progress, we must not allow our own inadequacies or delicate sensibilities to blind us during healthy debate. Our fragile egos sometimes keep us locked in the comfortable, familiar, and safe place of what we know; our egos have the potential to disrupt our perspective if we allow them. Passion is not insubordination just because others are uncomfortable with the dialogue. Good leaders know this; great leaders discern the difference and run to the dialogue in hopes of achieving what all leaders seek, collective buy-in for what they hope to execute.

I see that same fiery passion in my middle daughter, Sydney. She is like her father, but more like her grandmother, Rosa Lee Brown Harris. Just like me, Sydney is stubborn, but she wants to do good and give to others. I also see these qualities and experience them daily with my wife, Cynthia, who's an exceptionally smart, caring, genuine, and loving human being. She makes me look like a genius by sometimes pointing out my blind spots that I should consider. Truth be told, I am really not *that* smart. I'm simply a grinder who doesn't know how to quit. There are always others who are smarter and more talented than you. Our time here is short, and then we are dust. We exist for a speck of a moment in time. Then, we are gone forever. It's what we do in this brief moment through our service to others that will ultimately define our legacy, which cannot be erased or changed. It will endure through others forever.

As a leader, you are going to have to communicate with others. It comes with the territory. Becoming an effective leader requires conscious effort—especially around the skills that give us pause because we may believe they are not up to par. A leader does not have the luxury to simply say, "I don't do well in front of crowds" or "I prefer not to get to know the people reporting to me in order to maintain professionalism." These excuses constitute a significant business risk to the growth and momentum of an organization, team, or department.

On the other hand, getting too close to those who report to you is not necessarily the way to go. Being a strategic cog in the organizational wheel does not consistently lend itself to getting close to everyone. Friendship with all those you work with, for example, is an unreasonable expectation. However, great leaders can and do draw appropriate boundaries that are built on mutual respect, collective purpose, and a shared desire to build something together that far exceeds anything either party could achieve alone. These shared values foster conversations that create lasting momentum. It is going to be the uncomfortable conversations that move the needle.

I loved Coach Hamner. He was Coach Rut's most trusted assistant basketball and baseball coach. Coach Hamner had a sarcasm that matched his intellect—sharp, but not biting; smart, but not condescending—almost beguiling. I connected with him immediately. Coach Hamner took immense pleasure in watching us go through the Feast, but he was also our English teacher. He welcomed me into the Benedictine family as well as his own home. I immediately connected with the love his entire family gave me. His children were young back then, but I could feel their love. They were another family that stabilized my wayward soul.

Perhaps one of the most important things Coach Hamner gave me was the love of officiating basketball, which took hold even before I knew it. This journey began during my weekend visits home from JMU. I would referee the parochial school games comprised of little kids from seven to twelve years old. By far, my favorite games were with the first graders. They simply wanted to have fun and play. I smile when I think about how these energetic, smiling, excited little kids would just pick up the ball and run with it like a football, then slide around, falling to the ground, not yet in control of their coordination. They were adorable. I loved to work with these children because of their un-contaminated joy that just wanted to play—together. They had not yet learned how to be selfish. They only wanted to please those that mattered most. Even back then, I was keenly aware of this reality. It resonated with me, and I enjoyed watching them just have fun playing a child's game.

What I enjoyed most when refereeing games for young kids was when screaming, irate parents (confession: I was one of those when my children played, and *because* I had played and refereed, I believed I saw everything clearly) would give Mike F., my refereeing partner and close friend, a hard but enjoyable time. We allowed the kids to travel, slide around, double-dribble, and do all sorts of other illegal things, and we would not penalize them for it. The goal was for the kids to enjoy the game, have fun, and learn the rules, but not be so tightly bound to them that joy of the game was squeezed from their energetic and youthful spirits. We also would occasionally sprinkle some instruction into the game so they could learn and improve. The kids would smile and nod with every piece of direction, hungry for more and ready to get to the next play.

Whenever parents would get out of control, Mike and I would do one thing that *always* worked. A passionate parent (or set of parents) would be giving us the business on how we were missing fouls and letting the kids run around like a bunch of out-of-control maniacs. When we were fed up with the parents' shenanigans, we would blow the whistle, stop the game, turn to little Johnnie or Sarah, and say, "Hey, tell your parents to chill out. They're messing up *your* game." This always worked like a charm. The kids would turn to the bleachers and yell at the top of their voices, "Mom, Dad, please stop!" It was classic. Mike and I would look at each other with this cat-that-ate-the-canary look and wait for it. Complete and deafening silence would follow. The "good" parents would turn to stare at the "bad" parents with a look of disdain, as if to say, "Ooh, what are you going to do now except sit down and be quiet?" Watching the parents slowly sit down or calmly fold their arms in their lap, glancing around to see how many other parents were staring directly at them, was funny as hell. What made it all the more special was giving the kids an opportunity to shut the parents down for a change, which in those moments was a sight to behold. They loved it.

Their infectious smiles confirmed what Mike and I already knew. *Damn, that felt good!*

Invariably, after the game, the parents would come up to Mike and me to apologize for their behavior. We would graciously accept their apologies, but we'd also use this as another teachable moment and encourage them to apologize directly to their child. They always understood the message, took their humility medicine, and contritely apologized to their child. You could see the kids' confidence grow in that very moment. I loved this game and its ability to give small doses of confidence and humility at precisely the right moment.

I mentioned Coach Hamner and Mike because they are central to my basketball leadership journey. Coach Hamner introduced me to refereeing little kids to earn some side money on the weekends, but Mike introduced me to the love of officiating basketball. The funny thing is, at the time, I had no desire to get serious about refereeing. It was strictly a side-hustle. I was not interested in any long-term commitment.

Leadership Lesson Eight: Sometimes, your leadership path will unfold organically before your very eyes.

You as the leader must be open to acknowledging the alternate path's existence as very specific to your calling. Once it is acknowledged, you must then discern if this alternate path is going to take you where you want to be. Consider who you want to become as a person first and a leader second. Don't be quick to dismiss the unfamiliar. Sometimes you may have to work harder to convince yourself that your course is true, and then work toward that reality. Remember, haste can be costly, stubbornness can stifle, and fear can fracture your leadership aspirations. Courage, however, will conquer the demons of adversity that seek to thwart your every move.

From the very first moment I met Mike F., I liked him. His infectiously friendly and positive attitude and flaming red hair immediately put me at ease. His kind soul spoke to me. He loved basketball just as much as I did, if not more. What I would come to learn later as our friendship grew over the years was that he was also a talented and avid golfer. The dude could work a golf ball. Playing golf with Mike on several occasions years ago indirectly fueled some of my passion for the game to this very day. Watching him say, "Double H, I need to fly the pin and back that thing up," (spin the golf ball back toward the flagstick) or, "Double H, I need to fly this thing over that tree and drop it softly," then watch him do that very thing, was inspiring. I liked watching Mike navigate a golf course, and I would sometimes actually get to enjoy watching when I wasn't trying to recover from one of my own wayward shots.

Mind you, I am not a bad golfer. I'm around a ten handicap, which simply means that throughout the course of a round, I hit more decent shots than horrible shots. It's a very humbling game. It's another example of life personified through a sport most people will never master but simply enjoy. I hack it up and loose golf balls just like everyone else. However, with a ten-point handicap I will hit some shots during a round of golf that look like I should be on tour, and then on the very next hole, I'll look like I've never picked up a club before. That is the game as an amateur. One good shot within a single round of golf will give us joy. It's that one great shot that brings us back. I keep returning to it because of those fleeting but glorious shots that briefly remind me of how great it feels when all the minutiae of a golf swing align perfectly. I wish I could bottle that perfect swing of the golf club and repeat it over and over again—but instead, I often find myself occasionally searching the woods for a golf ball that wants to stay hidden because the golf gods know what they are doing. They also have a great sense of humor. Sometimes, as golfers know, you end up finding two or three golf balls to replace the one you just lost. Golf is a funny game—and maddening at times. Other times, I simply choose to let the wayward and disobedient golf ball remain lost and not give any energy to locating it. Drop another and keep it moving. Enjoy the game. That is why golf balls come in a three pack. Remember, that lost golf ball is actually for next hack like yourself who will come after you, hoping to find their lost friend.

The harmless but persistent hounding from Mike to officially get involved with learning how to become a high school basketball referee was an interesting journey for me. He never let up. Each weekend when I came home from JMU, Coach Hamner assigned me to work several games, each lasting about an hour. To a young college student home for the weekend, picking up an extra hundred or so bucks was a nice side hustle I could live with.

During each game, Mike would interject a friendly reminder: "Hey, Double H, you really should get serious about refereeing. You'd be great at it. You already know the game. It would be easy for you!"

I would look at him, turn my face up with a disdainful look

to say, "Nope. Side hustle, Mike. Quit asking. I'm not interested in making this something serious."

As determined as I was not to concern myself with Mike's persistence, he was just as determined to move my unresolved, youthful confidence—some would call it arrogance—with a desire he knew to be a pleasure I'd yet to experience. I loved working with Mike. He was an enjoyable, kind, and friendly pain in my ass. As with so many men in my life, Mike saw something in me well before I realized it. He knew something I would eventually come to understand. This was my game. She had found me long before I found her.

Chapter Seven

During my years at Benedictine under the tutelage of Coach Rut, Coach Hamner, Coach Sagester, Coach Clark, and others, we won several Virginia State Catholic Championships as well as the coveted Benedictine Capital City Classic (BCCC). This annual Christmas holiday tournament featured some of the most talented All-Americans from across the country, some of whom would become great college and NBA players. The BCCC is one of my favorite events of the year. It was a time when students, faculty, family, alumni, and friends would converge on this small yet somehow strangely sufficient rustic green barn of a gym to support a team of cadets swaddled in tradition, forged in sweat, and built on decades of allegiance to those who came before them. I vividly remember a section of the gym that was secured for the freshmen. They were required to stand for the duration of the game and cheer at the top of their lungs. They were glorious. They were maniacs. We were one team.

The four years I spent at Benedictine were literally a blur. One of my fondest memories, however, was that my granny was there to witness my graduation ceremony in our cathedral. Because Benedictine was a military Catholic institution, our ceremony back then was not the traditional walk-across-the stage-and-shake-hands-with-the-principal event. We had a mass, our valedictorian spoke, along with a few others, and then it was over. Just as quickly as my high school journey had begun, it was finished. It was time to move on. Another basketball floor was calling me; another coach to learn from; another soul would wonder, "Where in the world did this little pissant of a guy come from?"

My journey to James Madison University was a true love story in more ways than one. I'll start by telling you that favor isn't fair. It rarely is. Especially when you don't even realize it is upon you and there is nothing you can do about it—except maybe screw it up. Sometimes ignorance is bliss. I'll explain.

Although many members of my family had a significant impact on my life and development, it was my beloved granny, Cornelia Payne, who transitioned beautifully to her eternal resting place in heaven at her home amongst family and close friends at the blissfully youthful age of ninety-three that arguably left the most indelible mark upon my life.

Granny worked at a prestigious law firm in Richmond, Virginia, four blocks from Benedictine High School. I remember after I finished class and practice, I would stroll on over to the law firm in my military attire—spit-shined black shoes, polished brass belt buckle, and several book bags in tow—just to say hello to her before getting on the bus home to Big Red's and Charlie Brown's house, which served as my primary residence during my parochial and high school years. Granny was the custodian responsible for the care of the entire building and office staff. She was the cleaning lady. For thirty years, she cleaned and cared for the staff and the building. Everyone loved my granny. That grace and love was also extended to me as her grandson. She was part of their family, and so was I.

The office complex was a three-story, multi-roof brick structure that looked like a modest mix of Colonial and Victorian architecture. It was not a large office building by any means, but to me as a high schooler going to visit his granny, it was huge. I also enjoyed Christmastime, when they would put up a huge tree directly in front of the large window, which was so big it displayed the second-floor balcony staircase. I enjoyed the warm, friendly greeting I would get every time I opened the huge front door. Sitting behind the front desk was a lady whose name now escapes me, but her beautiful and loving smile never left me. She was one of the few people in the world (along with Granny, Aunt Sheila, Denise, and my half-sister, Sam) who would call me by my middle name, Edward. This lady greeted me a warm, "Hey, Edward! It's good to see you again! How was school today? I'll let Cornelia know you're here, or you can go on back." I would smile, grateful to be recognized by an adult and honored that I would know someone of standing in such a grand place as this. I was a kid, but she made me feel special every time I stopped by. It was cool.

I would head back to the kitchen, located in the rear of the building, where Granny was keeping everything spotless. She was always delighted to see me. We would chit-chat about school, people, basketball, and baseball. She loved baseball. Sometimes, knowing I was starving from a hard day of basketball practice, she would fix me something to eat and make me some outrageously sweet tea to wash it down.

Another fond memory I have of roaming this huge office

building was when Granny would allow me to go to the basement and read through the old law books that were stacked everywhere. The room was small, even back then, but I loved to just walk around, looking through statute law books. I know. We all have stuff that for whatever strange reason appeals to us. Statute law books appealed to me back then, and I would spend hours in that basement mesmerized by the sheer volume of legalese these lawyers were responsible for not only comprehending but mastering in its application for the benefit of others. Most of the content was, of course, foreign to me. That did not matter one bit. Reading it was somehow mesmerizing and strangely relaxing.

Let's fast forward to my senior year, about six months before my graduation. I had made up my mind that the school for me was James Madison University, located in Harrisonburg, Virginia, and surrounded with the picturesque backdrop of the gorgeous Shenandoah Valley. During one of our kitchen chats, I told Granny that I didn't want to go anywhere else, and I was going to play basketball at JMU. I was a decent point guard (I think second-team All-Metro), but I was not highly recruited and certainly not being recruited by JMU. I simply spoke into the atmosphere that I was going to play there, and that was that. This confidence willed me toward someplace, something greater than I could even imagine at the time.

Long story short, my granny, knowing my desire to attend JMU, completely unbeknownst to me, spoke with someone at the law firm who spoke with someone at JMU, who spoke with the president. At that, it was Dr. R. E. Carrier. I received an early admission letter from JMU (my grades and SAT scores weren't bad either) well ahead of most other students seeking admission to the college or university of their choosing. Keep in mind that this was over thirty years ago—1984 to be exact—and all I knew was that I was in the catbird seat while I was watching my classmates sweat it out on their first, second, and third choices. I was over the moon with gleeful excitement and anxious anticipation of what was to come. More than that, however, I was amazed at my granny's maneuvering. With less than a sixth-grade education, she was by far one of the most brilliant people I've ever known. I remember feeling as if I were floating on a cloud with that early acceptance letter in my hand, waving it as a flag of honor to anyone who'd read it. I was proud. I was also humbled that my granny had favor with people who believed in her and cared for her so much that they extended their grace and legal influence to a boy from the hood so he could continue his higher education. Yes, that is what true favor looks like.

I was not supposed to be there. An unimaginable sweven. Every other player was on an athletic scholarship, and they belonged there. No one invited me to become a part of this basketball team. I was invited to JMU to participate as a student, not an athlete. For that, I had to fight yet another battle for a different type of acceptance. I was not welcome in this exclusive fraternity of athletes. Nope. I had no shot. Zero. Walk-on, non-scholarship athletes thirty years ago were not the coveted entity they are today. Back then, we were a frowned-upon annoyance that made life more difficult for coaches who had to decipher yet another variable in their already exhaustive list of duties—not the least of which was winning basketball games that was a requirement to stay employed. Losing too many games, failing to compete for conference championships, and meeting inconsistent success costs coaches their jobs. I loved those odds. I cannot recall how many walk-ons there were, but I do vividly remember my focused anger. There was no way in hell I was going to not make this JMU men's basketball team. In my mind, dismissal from this extremely personal goal was never an option.

I remember Coach Campanelli as an accomplished Italian firecracker of a basketball coach who was on players' asses from the very beginning of practice until the very last drill. He was a taskmaster with his rolled-up program that had the entire practice schedule mapped out by the minute on it. I hated that program. The drills and endless exactness for punctuality seated itself deep within my soul and reinforced what was already familiar—repetition, hard work, and discipline. Remember, Coach Bernie built the foundation, while Coach Rut and Coach Hamner chiseled a better basketball player and person. Coach Campanelli was the sarcastic doubter that fueled my resolve. In my mind, that rolled-up program represented his plan to direct, drive, and sometimes torment us in order to bend the players to his will. I hated that rolled-up program.

Although I despised that program, one of the things I loved about Coach Campanelli was that he consistently recognized effort and hustle during practice. It didn't matter if you were a walk-on or scholarship athlete: he loved effort. That was my doorway. That was my welcome mat. I wiped my feet, turned the handle, stepped into the unknown. I was determined to outwork everyone else in this exclusive club. More than anything, I wanted their confirmation that I was good enough, that I belonged here. My mind was clear. I made myself comfortable with believing I was going to be a member of this team, even if Coach Campanelli and the other players hadn't realized it yet.

There was a mixture of curiosity and wishful thinking among the scholarship athletes who knew their positions on the team were already secured juxtaposed against the basketball wannabes striving for the coaches' validation. I took their passive-aggressive, uninterested body language as arrogance. Again, whether the arrogance was true or manufactured by my psyche is inconsequential. I needed something combustible. I found it in their polite dismissal of my basketball acumen. I used the fuel of their doubt to sustain me as the coaches, players, and other walk-ons looked at this diminutive kid with disdain, without any substantial evidence to support their flawed attitude that I was not worthy of this opportunity. All of the doubt from those more talented not only increased my will, but also kindled the fire of my ever-present anger. As I've mentioned previously, telling me I cannot do something—anything—is akin to placing a well-cured hickory log on my fire of faith and belief. The only thing left to do is watch it ignite and burn with an intensity that refuses to be extinguished. They did not believe I deserved the same opportunity that they sometimes took for granted, which manifested itself in occasional lackluster effort, a luxury they could afford. There were no reasonable accommodations here. It was simply a chance. I knew I needed to make the most of it.

I poured that focused anger and determination into every drill, sprint, dribble, pass, rebound, and defensive scrum. I was literally outside of myself watching myself do something not in my own strength. I was not here. I was another little kid, back at that cold barracks, hoping to get a chance to learn this fun game called basketball. And nineteen-year-old Harold was sitting in the empty stands of the expansive JMU Convocation Center watching all this play out right before me. It was surreal.

One of the most gratifying days of my entire basketball life came several weeks later, well into the try-out period. Most if not all of the walk-ons had been eliminated. Only one remained. Coach called me into the office before practice to have what I thought would be the defining chat that would confirm or possibly deny my vision—the chat previously delivered to the other clowns who'd also thought they had a chance to make this team. They also had a vision, a dream that they belonged here just as much if not more so than even me. This was it. I was the only clown left. As I made that seemingly long walk from the locker room to Coach's office, I remember thinking, *I did my best. I left it all out there on the court. I can walk away from this game with absolutely no regrets whatsoever.* I felt good about how far I had come. If this was going to be the final chapter to my basketball playing career, I felt good about how it was going to end.

I turned the knob to Coach Campanelli's door, and as I walked into his elaborate office filled with awards and memorabilia from years of coaching success, I was surprised at the look on his face. It was a mixture of dissatisfaction, pride, and confusion. I wasn't sure how to read it, but one thing I was certain of was that his face didn't say, "This is the end of the road for you and your dream of making this team." It was something very different indeed.

I loved the fact that Coach Campanelli didn't mince words. He was direct. He didn't waste time with talking around subjects.

His crucial conversations were directly in front of you, unmistakable and crystal clear. "Son, I've been trying to get rid of your ass from the moment you got here!" I will never forget those words. They were delivered with a clarity and conviction that cut me sharply but didn't penetrate my spirit. Why? Because when he uttered them, he was smiling. Sitting directly across from him, separated by only the huge desk, I felt immensely small and insignificant in his presence, surrounded by all of his coaching success and rich basketball history. Knowing that something important was about to happen but being unsure of what filled me with a strange confidence. Realizing that I had broken through this tough Italian's hard-nosed exterior as a new member of the team changed the paradigm and validated my commitment. I knew in that moment I was here to stay. I knew I had made it. My effort had been rewarded. Some of his words to other players at practices still reverberate in my soul: "Hey! How in the hell does a walk-on outwork you on a play you've been running for two years? This little pissant is kicking your ass! Wake up!" Again, this was fuel being poured into my tank—that left-handed compliment disguised as player rebuke. I drank it up. Every admonishment to the scholarship players that acknowledged how hard I was working to send the message that I was here to stay turned their not-so-subtle dismissive skepticism into genuine and sincere respect. I had won them over. If I never played a single minute of a single game, the currency of respect from much more talented players and the coaches' affirmation was all I needed. It was more than enough. It was everything.

Hearing Coach Campanelli describe in detail how he hadn't originally wanted me here and how I was only the second player ever to make the JMU men's basketball team as a walk-on (D. Steele was the first) was a huge accomplishment. I saw the pride in his face as he congratulated me for making the team. It was almost as if I'd endured his personal boot camp, his gauntlet, his survival island. As great as I felt about officially making the team (the entire team congratulated me in the locker room, and that was very cool, by the way. . . .) it was a bittersweet and very important moment in my life. I had made the team, but I was not going to receive a scholarship. Paying my way through college by stocking shelves at the local Food Lion and working in the mall at a retail clothier was how I paid tuition, along with Mr. United States "Pell Grant." It would have been nice to get a "full ride" scholarship that included everything: books, room and board, tuition, meal allowance, and the biggest perks of all—free sneakers and gear! However, I was going to remain a walk-on. There was no full scholarship in the cards for me.

Regardless, making the team was an awesome badge of honor bestowed upon those select few who earn a level of respect among the student population—especially those who were summarily dismissed by Coach Campanelli earlier. It was a badge I gratefully wore, not just for me, but for all those guys cut during the try-out process—the guys I would see playing recreational league or pick-up games in the auxiliary gyms at Godwin Hall, still sour that they hadn't made the team. There was no gloating, only respect for their hustle and their game. Some of the guys who got cut were much better than me, but the position they played was already occupied by multiple scholarship players. Sometimes, timing and luck smile favorably upon you. The other reason I didn't gloat was because of the support given to me by the players cut from the team. They cheered for me to win. I represented all of them who wouldn't get this chance. It simply said, "We did it! We made it, and there's no one who can take it away from us"— at least not that year.

I enjoyed my role as a practice player who was there to make the starters work hard, get better, and hopefully win games. As a life-long starter on every team I ever played on, learning now to be a benchwarmer was a role I took on with complete acceptance, not as a player defeated, but rather a player who understands exactly where he is and what he's prescribed to do. I worked my butt off. I stayed in my lane—effort, hustle, and a grateful attitude that I simply had earned "a seat on the bus."

Leadership Lesson Nine: Learn to stay in your lane.

Now, let's be clear. "Staying in your lane" does not mean never venturing into areas that don't fall necessarily in your wheelhouse. One of my best mentors once shared with me some very brief yet profound words that still resonate with me to this very day: "We have good people for that." There is nothing earth-shattering here except to keep in mind that as a trusted, competent leader, you should not be all over the map trying to do and know everything. I am of the opinion that is a losing proposition and a fundamentally flawed will inevitably leave you exhausted, insecure, frustrated, and completely in the reactive realm. The ability to properly assess talent is crucial here. Understanding what gaps need to be filled—and having the courage to make those changes—is how a leader should approach this time management leadership strategy. For senior leaders and those not tasked with operations, the operational space should be visited periodically, not lived in. Tactics and strategy are the calling cards for those entrusted to guide teams, strengthen departments, change organizations, and revitalize companies.

Perhaps my proudest and most defining basketball *playing* moment was during a JMU home game. The crowd was massive, and the stadium was packed to the brink of overflow. The JMU Convocation Center was rocking, and it was a blow-out. We were up by almost thirty points with about four minutes remaining, and the game was already decided. I don't recall the team nor does it matter, but the culmination of many hours of blood, sweat, and sometimes tears all came to a head in one signature moment when, unbeknownst to me, my then-roommates unveiled a bedsheet spray-painted with the message that read, clear as day, "Give this graveyard some life! play Harold!" The bedsheet was unfurled like the American Flag, clearly visible in the far end of the court on the second level. Everyone saw it and began to cheer, "We want Harold! We want Harold!" As embarrassed as I was, I was also filled with joy that manifested in a smile as bright as the sun. My teammates on the bench with me nudged me playfully as if to say, "Hey dude, that's for you!" As the chants grew louder, Coach Campanelli didn't flinch. With his rolled-up program, he simply kept coaching his players. He would stand up, bark out a play, admonish an official, and sit back down.

Then it happened. As the crescendo reached a fever pitch, I saw Coach get up, walk in my direction, point that lovely, rolled-up program directly at me, and utter the magic words: "Get in there for Rob." Rob was our starting point guard, and he was a strong, deliberate player who could be trusted to care for the basketball and run the team efficiently. Coach Campanelli hated self-inflicted turnovers—most coaches do. I did not want to get into the game and make a mistake with some bonehead turnover. My heart skipped a beat, and I tried to be cool about it. That didn't work. I was scared as hell and excited at the same time. When the crowd saw me get up off the bench, the entire place went nuts! I don't remember how much time was remaining, but I do remember putting the defender on skates with a behind-the-back move and taking a jump shot that unfortunately missed the mark. The move made the bench jump up out of their seats like today's teams when a teammate slams home a dunk and posturizes an unwilling defender. It was a cool moment, nonetheless.

Sometimes staying in your lane as a leader begins with learning how to be a willing and supportive follower. I learned how to be a follower when the team was invited to get our JMU brains beat out by one of college basketball's greatest and most storied programs. Traveling to the University of Kentucky to play in a Christmas tournament was also a cool experience. I got to see Claiborne Fame, home of the legendary horse Secretariat, where they still breed world-class racehorses to this very day. I also got the opportunity to play in Adolph Rupp Arena, which was at that time home of the Kentucky Wildcats. We were getting drummed by forty points, and there was less than a minute remaining. You may have seen it play out before—clean up time for the "scrubs," if you will. I simply relished in the moment. Part of being a great leader is in understanding the moment and knowing when to just be a good follower. Enjoying fifty-six seconds of participating in a game moment most walk-ons would die for was a great lesson learned during this time of my modest playing career. Truth be told, I was not impressed with the facility when I first laid eyes on it. It looked like a big, ugly warehouse with huge blue duct work; steep rows of hard blue benches stretched from the midsection of the arena to the ceiling. I remember thinking, "Damn, you'd fall over and break your neck if you stood up and looked down!" It was that steep. The big blue "K" in the middle of the court was neat to see and walk across. Suffice it to say that was one of the highlights—simply being there. We got smoked.

My basketball career would ebb and flow during the next four years. I'd return to play my sophomore year under a new coach, J. Thurston (Coach Campanelli headed to California Berkley). I liked Coach Thurston for several reasons. He had piercing blue eyes that resonated confidence. He also reminded me of my first coach, Coach Bernie. They were similar in physical stature and both passionate about the game. Coach Thurston loved that same damn rolled-up program! I liked him anyway. I didn't play my junior year because I chose to pursue other activities, including being the Black Student Alliance (BSA) President under to tutelage of a terrific mentor, Mr. Byron B., but on a dare, I came back for my senior year. It was mostly to prove that I still had it in me, and I could still play the game at Division I level. One of my few regrets was that I only took the team photo during my freshmen year and not the other years. Sometimes walk-ons didn't get that consideration. At that time the team photos were hung in the hallways of the Convocation Center. This seemingly innocuous photo that permanently documented my basketball journey would remain captured forever in an ordinary photo of a little dude who dared to dream—but to me, that picture was everything. There are other photos buried deep within the annuls of some photographer's collection that document my time as a JMU Duke basketball player, some of which I've had the pleasure to unearth and share with my family. It's like looking at another person who you vaguely recognize but feel incredibly distant from due to the road and years of mileage and experiences that now separate then from the now. For those memories that capture a moment in time, I remain grateful and humbled by the experience. They are reminders that I was there in both heart and soul. I loved the game, and it loved me back. That team picture was living proof of a dream fulfilled, a dream that would not fade or lose its luster over time.

That success would endure forever.

Chapter Eight

Basketball officiating has taken me on some exciting, disappointing, and wonderful journeys through the years. What started as an extra cash college hustle evolved into a love affair that has blessed me with connections to some wonderful people, places, and circumstances far beyond my expectations.

This game has given me and my family opportunities that warrant mentioning. This game put our oldest daughter, Jasmine, through college on a full athletic scholarship for which she successfully matriculated into two degrees, one in communications and one in criminal justice. (Go ECU Pirates!) This game also allowed Jasmine to travel the world and experience new cultures across globe from Puerto Rico to Poland. Believe it or not, in 2010, during my final semester of graduate school, my international trip was part of the VCU information technology management master's program, and Jasmine was playing for a Polish team at the same time. We were literally in the same country at the exact same time less than two hundred miles apart! We were scurrying about trying to manipulate our schedules to at least see each other, if only for a moment. I was in Warsaw, and she was in Bydgoszcz. We never could work out the logistics due to her basketball schedule and my cohort logistics, but for all of our wrangling, we understood the odds of that situation and how spectacular a coincidence it truly was.

As a parent, rooting for my children's success came easily, no matter their activity of choice. I rooted for their team and individual successes with intense enthusiasm and unapologetic vigor. As a basketball official, however, it was sheer torture. I am as complimentary of excellent officiating by others as I am critical. Now, here's a secret that most basketball fans who aren't officials don't realize: we are trained to watch a specific area, not the ball. Most people watch the ball everywhere it goes on the court. Their heads move around, scanning everything that we are trained to ignore. Now, that is not to say that officials don't get caught "ball-watching"—myself included. It happens. But in theory, officials are supposed to solely focus on their specific area—the technical terminology is "primary"—which simply translates to the uninitiated as primary area of responsibility. We also have "secondary" areas of coverage as well, but hopefully, you get the point—spectators watch the ball everywhere it goes, while we are trained not to. The three officials are focused on watching a particular area for a certain time frame. This is why you may see officials "rotate" their coverage or move into a better position so they can see what's happening in order to make the right call—or in some cases, the correct "no-call."

Nothing was more annoying while watching my children play than seeing a lazy basketball official who didn't properly position themselves to effectively referee during the game. Getting into the correct position to see the entire play start, develop, and finish significantly increases an official's call accuracy. Officials not working hard are easy to spot. Their posture does not project strength, their court presence is weak. They *look* like they know that they are doing, but their demeanor says they are not interested in the game but simply collecting a paycheck. Their mechanics are lazy when they report to the scorer's table. There is no precision in how they report events for coaches, scorer's tables, or players; they miss key game changes that require an understanding of game dynamics as well as the ebbs and flows of each team and its coaches. It drove me bonkers! Veteran officials much smarter and more successful than I have instilled deep within my officiating psyche the following simple, yet profound wisdom: "Officials miss plays for two reasons and two reasons only—1. They are out of position, and/or 2. They are surprised by the play." From the first time I heard those words uttered almost twenty-five years ago at a basketball officiating camp led by some of the best NCAA and NBA officials ever to set foot on a basketball court, they've never left me. They are true in their simplicity and yet complicated in their application.

We as officials are responsible for adjudicating the rules of basketball fairly and impartially without prejudice or emotional entanglement. Because we are also fallible human beings prone to falling prey to our emotions. Officials can very rarely miss the subtleties of the game that are clearly outlined in the rules but not necessarily observed until you have experienced the game situations as an official. Experience is sometimes the best teacher. Veteran official call this "seeing enough plays"—when you as an official have experienced different plays and situations enough times that they become normal to you, and the surprise element has been eliminated. Experiences of being in the fires of close games, buzzer-beaters that require monitor review, or a bang-bang play (official's terminology for plays that happen so quickly that if you're not in proper position so see it develop you can become surprised by the outcome) that can make the call of whether a team goes to the NCAA tournament or whether a coach and his staff are awarded a new contract. There is no teacher like experience. Experience can be as loving and kind as a second-grade school teacher or as brutal as a basic training military drill instructor. Our job is to let the players shine within the rules and stay out of harm's way. We are stewards of the game; people are there to watch the *players*, not the officials. A great game for officials is *not* being the lead story on ESPN's Sports Center and no one remembering who actually worked the game. Get in. Get out. Survive to referee another game. The fans are not there to see us anyway. They are there to watch the talent and skill of the athletes. The exceptional shooting, dribbling, and high-flying acrobatics that occasionally result in rim-rocking, spectacular dunks create memories that last a lifetime. Really good officials remember that.

Leadership Lesson Ten: Know the rules of the game you're playing.

These rules are critical to not only your personal success, but the success of the entire team. What's worse: not knowing the rules and making them up as you go, or knowing them but not applying them consistently? All three of these choices lead to a place filled with inescapable certainty if left as an unaddressed failure of mission. Leaders who don't know the rules are blindly navigating a minefield without the map that shows which steps to take and which to avoid. These rules are not written in any notebook that can be easily accessed. These rules are learned throughout your leadership journey. Once you learn them, you will not forget them, especially when they are painful administered through ignorance, arrogance, or simply poor decision making. Whatever the reason, lessons learned through discomfort are rarely forgotten.

Let's examine leadership that doesn't know the rules. You would think that during the interview process, some of the not-so-subtle yellow flags would appear. Red flag warning signs scream, "No! This person is not the right fit for this role." Yellow flag warnings don't scream, but they do signal that you should beware and ask more probing questions. Something may not be right here. Signs are often present, and we miss or choose to ignore them because of our visceral emotions. These feelings are so dangerous. They are not to be trusted solely by themselves. We've all done something just because it felt right in our gut, even when all of the empirical evidence suggested we should do otherwise.

After all the handshakes and pleasantries of the interview process are well behind us, the façade that was prominently on display for the interview slowly fades and is replaced by the real character. You've seen these people. You know exactly who they are. Sometimes, they can go a year or more before the mask comes off and colleagues begin to get a real sense of who the person truly is.

Then, the real question becomes: Why didn't we pay attention to the signs during the interview process or even during the probationary period in the first place? What was it about this so-called "leader" that had us captivated beyond our ability to logically see what was directly in front of us? What story did you tell yourself that created the blind spot that led to the decision to choose this leader over someone more capable who was a better fit for the organization? If you view yourself as a leader, only your journey can answer these questions for you. My crystal ball is currently out of commission. Do yourself a favor, though, and answer them. Ignoring these questions will leave you in a place of delusion reserved only for the completely comfortable who blissfully believe that all things will just magically work themselves out, even when they know their courage is in question and they choose to do nothing about it. Again, hoping things will simply improve is not a strategy. Sit with that for just a moment.

Leaders who don't know the rules or who are emotionally absent can be counted on to deliver chaos, the underbelly of a team trying to crawl out of the quicksand of mediocrity and misunderstanding. Another term used often for this is "arsonist." Now, we must be clear here. An arsonist intentionally sets a fire for the purpose of concealment or the destruction of the property of others. How does that look in today's business environment? Leaders who don't recognize the sensitivity a team may need run the risk of alienating themselves from the very group that can elevate them. Remember, you don't move the needle—you just think you do. It's your people who move the needle. The direction? Now, that one is all yours, leader.

Just like officials learning and studying the ever-changing basketball rule and case book, leaders must be dynamically adaptive. An exercise that may be of value is one that commits pen to paper for clarity. Here's what I mean. When you're unsure of the rules within your particular team, write down what you believe them to be, and then have an accountability partner (everyone needs at least one in their lives) go over them with you. This accountability gives you an indication of your potential vulnerabilities and prevents you from moving too quickly with misconceptions. Some folks might say, "Check yourself before you wreck yourself." Sometimes, we simply move too quickly. Your feelings, if left unchecked, can lead to some unintended consequences of poor decisions. Writing things down moves your tangled, confused thoughts into the realm of concrete application. I read a fortune cookie recently (Have I mentioned I *love* fortune cookies?) that said, "Writing is our thoughts clarified." I believe that to be true. Seeing it on paper is clarifying and motivational. Writing it down makes it real. It encourages you to take action. It creates momentum. Writing it down is liberating.

Leaders who don't take the time to at least get clarity on the rules of engagement force others to be at the mercy of their reactive decision-making, firefighting, and morale-deadening leadership. Nothing stifles momentum like a leader who doesn't even recognize they are leaving a plethora of professional carnage in the wake of what they believe to be the best strategic decision in the moment. Where's courage when you need it? More on that later.

Conversely, leaders who understand their strengths and weaknesses are enjoyable to work with. They get it. They understand the gravity of their limitations and walk with confidence into the newness of a vision that has yet to reveal its completeness. Their purpose is clear—right a ship, enhance performance, increase market share, change a culture, or improve customer satisfaction. Whatever the mission, they are up to the task because they understand the rules and how to play by them based on their own personal strengths and opportunities for improvement.

Excellent leaders surround themselves not with "yes people," but with people who will speak truth to them and are strong in the areas where they are weak. By surrounding themselves with strong and intelligent people who balance their strengths (some call these relationships "mastermind alliances" or "business coalitions"), an exceptional leader buffers the unintended consequences of those in their care and secures the unfortunate business situations that require intervention, delegation, or closer examination. They use all resources and talents at their disposal. They don't operate exclusively in the vacuum of their own leadership, position or privilege.

No matter the destination, we do not get there alone. You may become successful in some things, but I believe that the power of the universe will deliver us to true success when we are operating in exactly what we have been called to do. That place calls you when the clutter of daily life is overwhelmingly its loudest. The noise of the moment will attempt to distract you with the delights of the flesh—stuff. Material goods are the falsehoods of success that blind so many. The blindfold of the now and the immediate gratification of the moment is substituted for the eternal victory of knowing you operated in truth of gifts, not the desires of your flesh for self-seeking admiration. Your destiny is your entire story and everything that happens within it—good and bad. *Choosing* to walk in the truth of that story is ultimate success manifested in the individuality of you that no one else can replicate. A single leader—one person—can change an entire organization. One person can make the difference between mediocre, magnificent, miserable, and memorable.

Book II
Bow Ties

Chapter Nine

I love a sloppy double cheeseburger! I mean just as sloppy as you can make it. Lettuce, tomatoes, ketchup, relish, mayonnaise, sometimes onions, but for sure extra ketchup and mayonnaise. I am a true carnivore. Meat is what I enjoy. The juicy, savory flavor that comes from a well-cooked burger is, well, simply American. I also love a masterfully prepared medium-rare ribeye from time to time, but the juicy double cheeseburger gets me every time.

My love affair with the burger is directly tied to three signature personality traits that forever bind my story of perseverance to the present-day reality of what I believe to be my purpose. The first trait is courage. This is not a story of courage but rather a story devoid of it.

It was a signature moment as I sat there and watched my life unfold right before me. Being let go from a job after almost twenty years of service for being accused of stealing—an extra hamburger patty for my double-cheeseburger.

Yep, you read that correctly. What's interesting about this story is that the accuser, a cafeteria employee, was later fired for stealing. The cafeteria was inside my previous employer's building; they routinely contracted out the food services for the entire organization. This experience is mentioned not because of that devastating event that represented a signature moment in the overall trajectory of my life, but rather some key lessons and leadership takeaways that resulted from it.

One of those lessons is courage. Courage is acting in the presence of fear. Some leaders wilt under the weight of the moment. Some simply avoid it, hoping that it just passes them by without a scratch. Some leaders choose to embrace the moment and do what is not only right, but what is just. This is not one of those moments.

Getting fired was perhaps the *worst-best* thing that could have happened to me. Obviously, I did not at the time feel that way, but looking back on all of the moments, all of the turmoil leading up to that decision, all of the frustration from being silenced and relegated to responsibilities that felt more like an intern's—all these things brought back the feelings of anger I experienced as a child. It was a deep-seated sort of anger with the world that you cannot express in words, but only you know the penetrating, bone-chilling nature of its origin. I wanted to scream but couldn't. I wanted to yell out how unfairly I was being treated but didn't. I waited for others I trusted to come to my defense. I'd never experienced disciplinary action of any nature before, so the experience was completely foreign to me. I was lost.

What made matters worse was that I had genuine respect and personal admiration for the leader who was responsible for my growth and development at that time. I viewed him as extremely intelligent, practical, non-threatening, competent, and above all else, courageous. I believed that when the rubber met the road, he would stand up for me. He would defend me. He would protect me. My expectation was met with complete and utter disappointment. My heart was hardened, and my faith weakened.

It's funny how things shape us, shape our outlook on life

and how we view others and what they do to and for us at a precise moment in time. I have benefited from many outstanding leaders in my life who directly impacted my sensitivity to the professional and personal needs of others, but I am diametrically the polar opposite when it comes to having the empathetic gene. Now, some might call me a hypocrite at best or poser at worse, and I'd be the first to say that maybe they are right in some respects. Here's a perspective I'd like you to consider—the sympathy isn't what was being asked for in that moment—it was putting a stake in the ground and making a decision to NOT support an employee that had no record of behaviors that would cause pause, doubt, or misgivings about his character. The choice was made to go with the anecdotal information misrepresented to create a narrative that was not true. My leader at that time and others chose the path of least resistance against a career filled with service to others as well as the company mission. What they thought to be true from their lens started a chain of unforeseen events that proved to be life-altering blessings to so many others far beyond the walls of this one organization. Again, it was the best worst day ever. The power here is not in the moment, but in what's to come from the moment. That power would be the transformation that would occur several years later. I had no clue. Life is funny that way. This is a point where I must mention that even when I least expected it, others came to my rescue with a lifeline opportunity for which I and a slew of other professionals are eternally grateful. This is a special shout out to my friend and colleague, D. Ingram, President of Capital Tech Search, located in Richmond, Virginia. His team believed in me and helped me regain my faith in humanity, people, and my career. They are, in my opinion, one of the top IT staffing firms in the country. That endorsement was for you, the reader; as for me, the recipient of their grace, professionalism, and competence, they are *the best* IT staffing firm in the country. Period. Now, before we move forward, I would be remiss if I did not acknowledge a second IT staffing firm that has been just as substantial in my career and personal development, Core Consulting, led by one of my mentors, Mike Jones, and supported by a team of exceptionally skilled and care professionals. Mike and Don K., just know this work did not become reality without your incredible business wisdom and leadership influences.

Remember, we can't always carry our own water. We just think we can.

Courage does not have to be confrontational. It does not have to offend. It should not look for a fight. Courage is tied to its very close friend, truth. Together, they can create a pathway of solid footing. Alternatively, they can create a menacing quicksand when used for selfish motives. Used to teach and nurture, courage and truth can be two of the greatest assets a servant-leader has at their disposal. Courage used for good can transform a struggling organization into a colossal behemoth by creating the appropriate balance between service to others and professional accountability every organization strives to attain.

But where does courage come from? There are no easy answers here. Forget about the dictionary definition of the word for minute. What does true courage look and feel like to you? Is it speaking up when silence is preferred by the status quo because decades of experience tell you so? Is it being quiet when you should be calling attention to something, or is it understanding that sometimes a different mouthpiece may have a more favorable outcome? Is it understanding the moment and discerning the right time for engagement? I used the term "engagement" intentionally here. Courage is absolutely an engagement—an engagement in truth-finding. It's also a choice. Some leaders make the courageous choice knowing that the stakes are high, while others shy away from that mantle of very personal accountability. Cowardice comes to mind here, but plenty of other descriptions may be appropriate—maturity, experience, naivety, or blissful ignorance.

I'm going to stick with cowardice. That's just me.

This is the journey most great leaders embrace while the pretender avoids this trip for as long as possible, hoping that uncomfortable circumstances never call their name. Sometimes, if you look closely, you can see the sand resting on their shoulders from putting their heads in the sand and ignoring situations, hoping that they will simply disappear. Hope, you remember, is not a strategy worth investing your time nor energy in. Even when they shake it off, that familiar hiding place somehow finds them again when the moment becomes too large for them confront. The moment completely engulfs their tiny courage, which shrinks with every passing second. The sand is a respite, a false safe haven. Whether it's choosing not to be the bearer of bad news or making tough decisions, embracing difficulty requires the "c" word: courage.

In this warp-speed world in which many things are immediately accessible, experience, as we know, is also a wonderful teacher. Time becomes the x-factor that may impact the leadership learning curve. It has no bias and is not driven by pedigree. It operates in the crystal-clear lens of truth and consequence. Action and reaction come together to tell a story that will not be manipulated by person or circumstance. It will last. It will endure. More often than not, experience can guide us into properly evaluating the path chosen or business rationale selected, or it can lend itself to faulty decision-making that ignores the inevitable consequences that will be a result in either course correction or failure. The failure, no matter how difficult, invariably has a silver lining, some lesson which should be extracted from the event that can be used to help a leader become the best version of themselves. Arrogant, look-at-me leaders who believe it's all about them miss this nugget all the time. The courage to acknowledge and change course when necessary even with an experience that is comfortably familiar requires courage. The humble, service-oriented leader skillfully pivots when required. The bigger picture: mission success is far more important than their fragile ego.

The second signature trait this life-long journey of self-discovery and service to others has taught me that must be addressed is self-pity. This state of mind is miserable. Don't permit it to hang around for any extended period of time in your space. The degrees in which self-pity manifests itself is directly related to one's maturity level. Some would better recognize this state of mind without its mask of victim mentality. You may be nodding not because you agree with me, but because you are seeing someone specific in your mind's eye. As people first and leaders second, being critical of others comes easy for us all occasionally, but it's only when we begin to see our own shortcomings that we truly begin to understand and appreciate where others may be in their journey. Walk a mile in the shoes of those you wish to judge before mentioning that you are indeed wearing the wrong shoes.

Self-pity took a deep hold of me during that tumultuous 2007 period in the Valley of Despair. I was under the illusion that this company owed me something. They owed me loyalty. After all, I'd been loyal to them for six months shy of twenty years—working overtime whenever it was asked, moving from department to department. I was pissed. I also learned that I was a terrible poker player, which did not help matters at all. The lens from which I viewed everything happening to me was out of focus, cracked, and not aligned with reality.

This is exactly what self-pity does to you—it blinds you and confuses you. I had never been fired from anything before. What in the world was going on here? Combine that self-pity with anger and a misplaced sense of entitlement, and there you have it—the dude we all love to hate. I was not a fun or happy person back then, but I was there, stuck in that quicksand of despair, and unable to find my way out. Was I completely broken and defeated? No. Not even close. The most heart-wrenching conversation in my mind was years behind me. Left in a destroyed bedroom of broken mirrors, ripped clothing and a river of tears and screams when my grandma told me that my mother was dead. No, this getting fired over a hamburger patty foolishness was minuscule by comparison but monumental in its impact upon my life, nonetheless. I felt in this moment of my dismissal that I was being taught a lesson. Sometimes in leadership life and the experience we get from trying to navigate through it are unrelenting and unforgiving. This experience was not about to compromise with me, make a deal with me, or feel sorry for me. In this moment, just like in life, I had to decide if I was going to be defined by the moment or if the moment was going to define me.

Sink or swim? Some leaders call theses crucible moments, career-defining situations, decisions that forever will represent your personal legacy long after the events are nothing more than an afterthought.

I chose the former. It really wasn't even close. The latter had no place in my psyche to germinate. No place to take root. No place for nasty character traits synonymous in their breeding to linger. Complicit in their negative results. Unbeknownst to me during this time of growth was the sneaky infiltration of one of the greatest enemies to us all. That third character trait that makes up this curious trifecta. This enemy snuck into my camp, pitched a tent, made a campfire, unrolled its bed, and set up shop. Because I was so trapped by the quicksand and stuck in my feelings, I never saw this demon appear—until it was almost too late. Bitterness was its name. Complete and total destruction was its aim.

Leadership Lesson Eleven: Don't ever allow the root of bitterness to enter your heart as a person or as a servant-leader of others.

Bitterness will destroy them first, you second, and the organization third and most profoundly.

Bitterness destroys others first due to the shattered dreams and crushed professional aspirations you will inevitably scatter all across the road on your way to what you think is the right leadership decision. It is the case that you are destroyed first. Others get the brunt of your clouded and misplaced judgement. Sometimes, you figure out how understanding the needs of others first may be the best course of action before it's too late. Sometimes you don't. How does bitterness manifest itself in our professional environments? It may look like a petty slight from a co-worker, a fractured word meant but not received in jest, an inappropriate comment publicly spoken but never rectified privately, a missed promotional opportunity, or worse, the promotion of the completely wrong person for the job that you believed was meant for you. It was never meant for you. What is destined for you has your name on it and will only be delivered to your address in the appropriate season, not to anyone else. It's a valuable lesson worth learning early in life, not later. Whatever the perceived rationale, bitterness is a slow poison that kills from the inside out. It seeps deep into the bone marrow from which there is no easy escape. The decisions made during periods of unexpected turmoil can be catastrophic, or they can be a monumental blessing. How do you know the difference? The outcome will tell the story.

What started as a love for burgers had turned into something totally unfamiliar to me—an assault on my character. An attack on the person I knew myself to be, as well as who I was not. This journey through that moment was somehow misconstrued and miscommunicated in order to make decisions for my dismissal easier for others to live with.

Back then, I was afraid of the unknown. I was unsure how

twenty years had passed so quickly, but I recognized it was now gone forever. Comforted by the many fond memories of my first foray into the world of IT, I think back on how it all came to be. . . .

Chapter Ten

I'll never forget my first day on the job, June 12, 1989. I was twenty-three years young and fresh off my first part-time job out of college, where I taught a basic computer typing course to ninety-seven juniors and seniors while coaching JV basketball for my high school alma mater, Benedictine Preparatory Academy.

His name was Al F. I liked him instantly. He was a white man over forty, with kind eyes and a friendly disposition. Al was one of the telecommunications managers in the IT department sent to welcome this totally green twenty-three-year-old professional wannabe who didn't know anything but believed he could conquer everything—a blissfully blind yet eager youth hungry to call himself a real working man. He greeted me warmly at the front desk and walked me down the hall to the telecommunications department. I remember fondly to this very day thinking to myself during the hall walk, "Man, I wish I could skip ahead five years and know where everything was and no longer have to ask anyone for directions to this or information about that."

It didn't take long. Several months earlier, an idea had dropped from the heavens into that Benedictine classroom. I realized I should hand out my modest resume to all my students, hoping that decision would garner some interest from just one kind soul who would give this youngster a chance. That singular thought was delivered to me by an angel that many years later remains a pleasant mystery I prefer to not untangle but to simply accept as universal favor upon my life. With the help of many strangers that would in time become colleagues and even true friends, my journey has been crafted into a successful thirty-two-year IT career filled with a lifetime of service to others for causes far greater than I.

Sitting at my teacher's desk in the early fall of 1988, staring at twenty-three high school teenagers, grading their typing and keyboard exercises—this was my initial introduction into the modern-day workforce. Although I had two part-time jobs that financed my education, this job with my high school alma mater seemed more professional. More real-world, with more of an "if you don't work, you don't eat" type of seriousness to it. After graduating from JMU in August of 1988, I went back to Benedictine as an enthusiastic and passionate part-time student worker who also had the responsibility of head JV basketball coach. I was basically twelve minutes older than most of those kids, but they were nothing short of professional and consistently addressed me as "Mr. Harris." It was rather uncomfortable at first. But before too long, truth be told, I came to enjoy the small modicum of respect given me by these future leaders.

The job didn't pay much—less than ten thousand dollars annually—but I was a working man learning to make my way in the world without the assistance of my immediate family. My roommate Mark, or P-Nut as we called him back then, was one of my closest childhood friends, handled his own business, and together we managed the rent for our modest two-bedroom apartment. Life was good.

Then came the call to the school office. Budget cuts and enrollment shortages for the upcoming year translated into part-time help being eliminated. And just like that, I was going to be out of a job. The saving grace for me was that this decision was made almost six months before school actually ended, so I had some time beat the street and get busy looking for a real job.

Looking back on this time, I have an even greater appreciation for the favor resting upon my life that contributed to the shaping of my leadership journey. Walking back to my classroom after that office budget meeting was difficult. I felt like I had just been kicked in the gut. I was relieved but scared at the same time. I was young and totally ill-equipped to handle the punches of life that, although they're extremely uncomfortable in the moment, are ultimately designed to shape your character and strengthen your resolve. I can assure you that in that moment I was not enjoying having my character shaped. I thought I was cool, trying not to display the nerves that come with adult responsibility, but I was far from okay. I was now twenty-two years old, about to turn twenty-three, and had never been on a real job interview. Now, I had to craft a presentable resume and apply for jobs by poring through newspaper job ads or seeking word of mouth solicitations. There was no social media in 1989, no internet job-searching juggernauts. No, I had to beat the streets, and doing so was a part of my character development that I faced with a confidence steadied by the hardships of my past. Was I scared of the possibility that I may not find a job and would end up out on the street? Yes, but I had a couple of things going for me: youthful conviction that I could do anything, and the courage to press on despite my fear. One of the reasons favor—spiritual intervention designed to impact your journey without your fleshly intervention—does distribute itself fairly among everyone is that not everyone *believes* in their heart that receiving favor is indeed possible. Anything is possible to those who believe it.

Sitting there, watching my students type away, I was lost in my own daydream about what the future would hold for my life—when it happened. I felt a raindrop of a thought that to this very day I cannot claim as my own, a nugget that would change the course of my life. I will never forget it.

"Dude, ask these kids if they would like an easy 'A' for this course and give your simple yet somewhat accomplished resume to them and instruct them to pass along to their parents. Most of these kids' parents will remember you from when you went to school here. Do it. Trust me. It will work out."

And just like that—my first foray into network marketing. I quickly handed out ninety-seven resumes to six classes of students who were marginally interested but quite enthused about the improved grading opportunity, unsure what the results would be but somewhat amused with my newly discovered networking creativity and underdeveloped faith.

About three weeks later, one of my students, Lee, came back with a message. "Hey, Mr. Harris, my dad wants you give him a call."

I was like, "Who's your dad?"

The student replied, "He's an IT Director for HealthNet." HealthNet was the IT arm of what is now Anthem Blue Cross and Blue Shield.

That meeting with Lee's father, Dick, and his telecommunications director, Chester, changed my career trajectory in more ways than I can count. My degree from JMU was in public administration and political science with a minor in economics. I knew absolutely nothing about telecommunications. I knew even less about information technology, but it did not matter. I would soon learn the reality of the age-old adage, "It's sometimes not about what you know, but *who* you know and *when* you know them. Sometimes, timing is everything. This was one of those moments. These two polished professionals sitting across from me looked like the photo of the Marriott father and son that is prominently displayed in the lobby in just about every Marriott Hotel in the world. Dick was sitting down, and Chester was standing behind him—at least, that's how I remember it because the Marriott thing immediately came to mind when I walked into the office. The next time you see that picture—or if it's the first time you ever see it—you will understand exactly what I'm talking about. That wry smile on your face will signify your connection to what I was experiencing in that moment now several decades ago.

A couple weeks later, I received an offer letter in the mail. I was going to be rich! They offered me about twenty-four thousand dollars per year. I'd never seen that much money attributed to me ever! I was over the moon with excitement, gratitude, and genuine surprise. Life was moving fast. I was enjoying the ride. Favor ain't fair. I was offered a job in an industry in which I had zero experience or qualifications. Dick and Chester took a chance on me. They gave me an opportunity. They gave me a shot to make my way in this world as a responsible, working professional. To this very day, I am grateful for their courage and kindness.

As a leader, their gesture to reach down and uplift a young kid fresh in his professional career has shaped my compassion for the human condition in an industry led by ones and zeros—on or off, and a ton of industry acronyms that care nothing about you and your feelings. A router is either routing traffic correctly or it isn't. A phone either has dial tone or it doesn't. Software is working properly or it's not. Technology doesn't care that you haven't slept in twelve hours, or that your dog ate your graduate dissertation. Technology is a specialized endeavor. It's either working or it's not. Technology, despite its ability to make our lives simpler, can often be strangely cold in its application. Caring for people and their successes resonates with me to my very core because of the generosity of others who saw something in me that I did not see in myself—the capacity to engage with something completely foreign and come to make a pretty good living at it with focused resolve and the counsel of others. Yeah, favor is awesome—even when you don't realize it's upon you until situations unveil themselves that help you understand how truly blessed you really are.

I would later come to find out that both Dick and Chester were also Benedictine graduates. Go figure. They took care of one of their own. I remain forever grateful to both men, one for his willingness to take a chance on me. The other, I am grateful for his teaching me the value of hard work and persistence, encouraging me to accept failure as an integral part of the journey, and demonstrating the importance of writing as a means of communication. That last one is still subject to interpretation and ongoing exercise but suffice it to say I am eternally grateful to Dick and Chester for all of their support and guidance. I experienced the benefit of not only excellent leadership early in my career, but

exceptional servant leadership with stewardship and professionalism tacked on for good measure.

Leadership Lesson Twelve: *Your journey is not yours alone.*

You cannot get to your destination all by yourself. Your boot-
straps aren't that long. Others will help you. Also remember that
others will attempt to stop you. Still others will protect you.
Smart leaders embrace the experience of others and leverage the
voices of their colleagues to increase their leadership perspective.
If you as a leader surround yourself with a bunch of 'Yes' men and
women you will eventually end up with a large group of stalled,
frustrated professionals who have absolutely nothing of value to
say. This kind of silence is deadly; it's a slow poison you as their
leader never see coming. Encourage banter and stimulate conversation not by *saying* you want people to speak up but by demonstrating the behavior that is complimentary, not contradictory,
to your words. The second you decide you don't like something
simply because it doesn't make you all warm and fuzzy, and then
go on to chastise or ridicule the source from whence it came, you
stifle the very momentum created by encouraging cooperation
between different perspectives. This particular example speaks to
an issue mentioned in previous chapters—the dreaded insecurity
rooted inside you, which is fear. It has a way of perpetually bind-
ing you to a faulty belief system that forces you away from the
very people placed in your path to help you.

This is why courageous leadership is such a tremendously important personal character trait. People say, "Be careful; you don't
want to die on that hill!" I get what they are attempting to convey
by this cautionary instruction—be careful about the battles that

you want to engage in—but damn it, if we are not going to stand up when we see something amiss, then when are we going to do it? When it suits our sensibilities? When it's politically advantageous? When? At what point are we willing to commit to the right thing to do because it is simply the right thing to do, no matter the cost?

That's just it: the cost. I get it. Most folks don't want to pay what's required when it has to be paid. They want to pay what they want to pay when and if they even want to pay at all. Sometimes that's very little. Most of the time, it's nothing. They want to get away scot-free. Strong leadership requires conviction forged in belief of purpose and cause. Courage is the outward expression of that inward foundational component secured through experiences both good and bad. It is acting in spite of the fear that cripples so many. Psychological, physical, or emotional trauma can cause courage to disappear like an alluring mist, here for just a moment and then gone forever.

Foundational core competencies for leaders are forged through repetition, situational experiences unfamiliar to their normal for which they are either stretched or broken in order to be reshaped into that leader, a better version of themselves. The initial part of that journey for some begins in terror. "Terror" would certainly describe the very first time I was introduced to a telecommunications voice and data wiring closet. I was expected to quickly learn how to wire closets like this one directly in front of me with relative ease and flawless execution. I was *so* not a fan. The immense and very intimidating wiring closet did not care one bit about my anxiety.

"Sunny—blue, orange, green, brown, slate, white, red, black, yellow, violet. Memorize it and never forget it. These are your primary and secondary colors. Try not to screw this up." Steve V. was his name. He was one of my very first technical field engineering supervisors, and he was a stud in my book. With a gazillion years of telecom and networking experience, Steve was sharp-witted, athletic (he and Mike F. both introduced me to the world and love of golf), and a terrific teammate and telecommunications supervisor. Long before I showed up on the scene, Steve already had twenty years of experience in the telecommunications industry. He knew the ins and outs of every voice and data closet in all of our buildings and surrounding offices. He knew what had been wired, rewired, cut, or moved, and where every piece of vendor equipment was stored. He was simply the guy who, if you didn't know the answer, would bail you out. I was very impressed with Steve's telecommunications skill and experience, and his willingness to teach me the technical side of the business.

I was even more impressed with Steve's ability to drive a golf ball. When Steve took out his driver I simply stood still and watched in amazement. He had a beautiful and rhythmic golf swing, but it wasn't his swing that mesmerized me. It was the uncannily consistent trajectory of his golf ball. During his tee shot at contact, the ball would always leave the golf tee and stay very low, almost parallel to the ground, and then about fifty yards out, it would magically rise toward the sky like an airplane taking off. It was a sweet sight to behold! Sometimes I'd make him (not that he wasn't a ham, by the way. . . .) hit another ball just so I could see him do it again. He'd chuckle and kindly oblige my request.

He always called me Sunny or "young fella."

"Young fella, you think you're an athlete? Let's see if you can work with this." He would hand me a golf ball, and before long, I was hooked. Steve was a good man, colleague, husband, and friend who is truly missed by all who knew him. Some people are just nice to be around because of their energy and infectious goodness of spirit. That was Steve V.

We started this journey with repetition because that is the lesson Steve drilled into my young soul. I can remember hours upon hours "cutting down cables" in the closets and floors. Voice and data cables were everywhere. Back then, Category 3 or CAT 3 cabling, as it was called, was all the rave back then and fiber optics was a new, exciting and mysterious technology being unwrapped at warp speed. Repetition not only strengthened my proficiency, but also weakened and subsequently destroyed any anxiety around operating in this new space. Practice! Yes, we're talking about practice! Thinking back on those days long gone, I can recall the booming voice of my grandfather reverberating through my mind as he told me on more than one occasion, "Boy, you can do it right or you can do it again!" This particular quote came flooding back to me one year when I was working in a floor trough, cutting down a bunch of data and voice cables for one of the many new cubicle installs and personnel relocations that would occur when new work spaces were being created. I was several years into the telecommunications job by then and had a pretty good idea of what I was doing—or so I thought.

Not so fast, my friends.

I had just "finished" wiring six different locations in these floor troughs, and my back was killing me. I had to sit on the floor and bend over to not only get to the cables, but maneuver them in such a way as to properly fit on the wood frame and six-ty-six block. I was proud of the work I'd done.

One of our lead technicians, John S., who also happened to be a Benedictine graduate, was standing over me, watching me complete the wiring assignment. John was a solid technician and an even better person. A quiet giant, if you will. He could see my obvious pride in what I thought was some quality work. He asks, "Harold, how's it coming? You all done?"

I proudly looked up at him from the floor and said, "Yep! We are golden!"

I'll never forget the following quote as long as I live. I occa-sionally use it today when the company and situation dictate. It's not a quote for public consumption.

"Don't piss on me and tell me it's raining!" said John. "That ain't rain! Do it again."

Boom! I was way past disappointed and pissed and on to hurt and anguish. That quote stung and shocked me like a bucket of ice-cold water dumped on me after a long hot run. I was very uncomfortable. The look on my face must have been hilarious because he burst out laughing. This was *so* not a laughing matter. What I thought was quality work was just okay. It wasn't excel-lence. I took shortcuts, and it showed. That exercise in repetition and quality ensured that from now on I'd do it right the first time—not do it over. It's funny to think back on it now, but at the time, not so much. This was a wonderful lesson for the young fella, one I've never forgotten. Very well done, John S. Thank you, sir.

Blue, orange, green, brown, slate, white, red, black, yellow, violet. I smile even now, remembering days long gone but secured by the many people who shaped my development technically, personally, and professionally. What may appear daunting and impossible in the moment is nothing more than a placeholder for the present. What's key is not allowing the present to be held hostage. You don't know that you can't do something if you've never even attempted it. Moving past the awe and fear of all those colors having to be placed in exact locations—every single time—was not an exercise that I would be held hostage to. Once again, repetition and determination to confront my shortcomings and move past them would be the mission. Failure, although not considered during my training, was a temporary, and sometimes quite necessary, stop in the learning process—not the final destination.

Leading others is a practiced discipline. It is a skill honed through humility and genuine concern for others. Being committed to the successful transformation of another into what they want rather than what you want them to become will not be sustained through misplaced ambition, character assassination, or political maneuvering. You will not be fully rewarded for disingenuous and political games designed to strengthen your professional position if you forget about all of the people who helped get where you are in the first place. Your continued elevation will be cemented in how well you continue to assist others in getting what they want. Sure, you may see some temporary successes, but just like the new employee becoming comfortable with their surroundings, the uncaring leader not concerned with the plight of others will relax, and eventually the true person will emerge. The proxy will permanently leave the building, and the essence of the real character will unveil itself.

The satisfaction that gives the true servant leader those visceral responses that come from the personal cycles of investment of time, energy, knowledge, and constructive feedback; from mentoring through the storms of chaos and confusion bound with moments of adulation and success associated with a job well done, is immeasurable. Then we rinse and repeat. This is how we learn. This is how we grow. This is how we help others. This is how we serve.

Chapter Eleven

I would describe my journey through life, IT, leadership, transition, and personal development as "unconventional." Everyone has a story to tell. That is what makes our individual travels a fascinating canvas that only we can paint. No other person on the planet can do what you do. Run to that truth. Embrace it. Be freed by it. If you are prone to self-doubt, don't allow yourself to be held hostage to your tiny—yes, tiny—fear of the potential failure that awaits you. Tell your story. Others need to hear it.

Artful storytelling is a skill worth investing in. Some leaders are natural storytellers, while others struggle to connect the dots. Natural storytellers quickly recognize how the moment may sometimes require a "connector" to solidify the message. The really great leaders use these moments as teachable mentoring opportunities to influence a particular skill or behavior. Some wonderful storytellers from American history are King, Roosevelt, Obama, Angelou, and Lincoln.

Time spent storytelling is not a wasted endeavor. These focused moments can be used to strengthen the core fibers of people, teams, and organizations. Being able to weave a story into an existing conversation is an artful talent that today's industry pioneering leaders understand and skillfully use to their advantage when crafting a narrative.

Word of caution: Be careful with going overboard by not

understanding the moment properly. Once, I witnessed a senior executive attempt to repeat a totally inappropriate story fit only for the boy's locker room and definitely not an all-hands-on-deck departmental meeting. You could literally see the momentum—their credibility and attendees' interest—leave the room. Nothing drains team morale more that the repetitive story being told for the millionth time to the same group of professionals that have already heard it before. OMG! You might as well put on a sign that says, "Here I come. You've heard this before, but please act like it's new!" What are the chances folks will remain engaged? You guessed it: slim to none.

Impactful leadership is not about entertainment. Professionals don't want to be entertained. They want to be inspired, heard, collaborated with, and challenged to truly make a positive difference. Inspiring others through storytelling requires true passion and enthusiasm that is not always seen in today's leadership circles. Leadership has become stagnant and careful, almost timid. Crucial conversations—uncomfortable dialogue that has the potential to put you at risk professionally and politically—are limbs most people don't want to venture out onto for fear of being unable to make their way back because the limb of safety was broken. It's important to understand that not every conversation is a crucial one that requires career-altering decisions. However, some conversations will lead to crucial and fruitful dialogue *if* both parties are willing to be honest about what's important to each of them.

Because, by its definition, you cannot engage in dialogue on your own, it's important that you surround yourself with people you can trust to be honest for the sake of the greater good. After success is met, conflict will most certainly follow. It is part of the evolution of accomplishment and progress. When conflict appears, try modifying your perspective to see it as a potential friend and not necessarily an adversary. People avoid conflict not only because it is inherently uncomfortable, but because they want to select the other road more traveled—the road they already know, that sandy road riddled with insecurity and marked with the familiar hole in which to bury their weary little head.

Forsaking your value system and overall sense of self cannot be usurped by someone else's unreasonable expectations of you. You can choose *not* to speak your mind or talk about things that matter to you. There is a right place and time for all things, but purposely prioritizing yourself below someone else's agenda at the expense of your voice is not a sustainable personal formula for your success. Resentment will rear its head eventually. We accomplish more by incorporating many varied opinions, skills, experiences, and value systems that weave the collective mesh of our strategic roadmaps. Regardless of your level of expertise or professional standing, your abilities significantly outweigh your deficiencies——no matter what your perceived deficit.

Let's say you've identified something you're not particularly good at; a professional skill gap. Public speaking comes to mind. For some, this is a terrifying experience. It can create such a visceral response that can completely paralyze even the best of us. Whatever your deficiency, whether perceived or real, own it and begin taking action to strengthen it. It's not okay for you as a leader to simply wallow in your weak spots. As a leader, you have a responsibility first to yourself, to be the best you can possibly be, and next to those whom you are charged to protect and nurture. By pushing through that which is uncomfortable, you begin the see the all the newness of the completely unfamiliar unfold right before your very eyes. Not only does your confidence grow in the moment, but so does your maturity as a leader.

In information technology, most employees eventually have to decide if they're going to remain in the technical realm or venture out into the abyss of human capital management. Some are even skilled enough to do both, so they manage personnel while staying connected to the technical world from which they originated. My hat is off to them. Some people are so management-averse they automatically equate management with non-stop drama. Management and the pursuit of leadership responsibilities *are* dramatic, but there is also so much more! It's accomplishment: destinations achieved that were previously thought unreachable, career growth positioned for new duties, and responsibilities never before imagined. Managing and directing people who trust you and want to succeed for the good of the team is a joy that every leader should be so fortunate to experience in their leadership journey.

For some, this journey of self-discovery can be quite daunting. Others make the transition rather seamlessly. Some never make it all. There is no wrong choice here. Learning what works for you is part of the journey. Some people confidently understand that they love the technical ones and zeros that the job presents—no ambiguity whatsoever. It's either on or off. Open or closed. Specific IP addresses. Exacting configuration of a router, switch, or server. Comfort lies in the exacting nature of the technical world.

The "behind the curtain" work that technicians, engineers, and administrators conduct every day is without question the evolution of the world in which we live. Most customers are not privy to the precise nature of how their devices work, nor do they care. They simply want things to work easily and reliably. The evolutionary speed of improving technology is only surpassed by the ingenuity of the next invention or process breakthrough. We are wired to improve for the next generation, whether we choose to believe that or not. Some keep their shovel in the technical realm. It's their sandbox. It's the space that they have chosen to play in and perfect.

Human capital management is a completely different beast altogether. Having quality leaders in your space, along with mentors committed to your success, is critical.

My love for the power of the analogy and storytelling comes directly from a man who I thought was as smart as they come. His name is Joseph W. He was a numbers guy who was also gifted with storytelling and analogy. I remember him as extremely practical and rarely excitable; always calm, cool, and deliberate in his speech; always in control of his message. He was an artful storyteller. Utilizing analogy to help people visualize his message, Joe could masterfully galvanize a group into quickly understanding even the most complex material.

You might think a numbers guy would be boring. Nope. Not this dude, at least not to me. He was not only meticulous, but he was funny as hell. When I went to him for counsel on my career aspirations, I was always met with enthusiasm, humor, and insightful conversation. He aimed not to influence my decision-making, but rather to expand my understanding of what

I wanted to do. He would talk through hypothetical situations using analogies to help put different factors in perspective. He was simply a fun person to talk with. It's nice to have people like that in your space. They want nothing from you. They have your best interest at heart. People will galvanize around this type of leadership. They will become solidified in their common purpose. This is a triple win—team member, leader, organization. The team member wins because they are more engaged in the collective good of the organization when they can see their role inside it; the leader of that team member wins because they have poured more fuel into the gas tank of the now supercharged team member who is committed to the leader and buys in to where the leader is headed; and finally, the organization wins because they now have two team members rowing in the same direction—not to mention, both members will likely stay within the organization rather than leave and take their talents elsewhere.

Some people call these artful management tactics "soft skills." Some leaders don't have a lot of trust in the process of building people. Ultimately, that is what true leadership is about: building an organization with others who strengthen the team goals and strategic direction of the leader. The interesting takeaway from witnessing this behavior over the years is that no leader has ascended to any level of responsibility without the benefit of another leader or several leaders who have invested in improving those soft skills. None of us wake up one day and simply understand a P&L statement, a cost-benefit ratio, ROI, or how to improve human performance through nurturing counsel and mentorship; goal setting; locating that nugget of intrinsic motivation nestled secretly behind unearthed doubt and fear masked as apprehension or dismissal. Inspiring others past that comfortable boundary of the familiar while forging excellence with your example demonstrates your commitment to the good of the team through successful service to the mission.

Empowered people move the needle in your favor. Multiple bootstraps are required. Yours's alone are simply not long enough.

Chapter Twelve

Most people move from desktop IT field services into some type of engineering role. Not me. After counsel with "Mr. Analogy" himself, I knew my path would include other people. I did not want to be kept "behind the curtain" like many other IT professionals. Joe not only helped me figure my path out, but encouraged me to engage in dialogue with other decision-makers. This route laid a workable foundation for me to achieve, even though they couldn't understand the unconventional move at the time. The "why" didn't make sense for them. By talking with other technical team members and people in management positions, I was able to clarify my direction based on their insightful perspectives and sound advice. It's nice when you can trust others who have only your best interest at heart and can help clarify your purposeful direction. Again, we don't get anywhere meaningful without the help of others who not only believe in your vision but also, and most importantly, believe in you and your unique talents and gifts. Remember leadership lesson one: the speaker really does matter.

Some of the paths you're going to travel will evolve completely on their own. They will unfold right before your very eyes. Others may not see the path or even believe it exists, for that matter. Keep going. Keep moving. Remember, your destination is yours alone. When needed, opportunity will properly align your journey with necessary people, situations, and talent for successful execution in the moment.

This does not mean you are alone. What I mean here is that you do not have to be confused by recommendations from people who cannot or will not see what has been revealed to you. Please remember that during your journey there will be times when other people simply cannot see what you see. They don't have the discernment to understand what is truly happening in the moment. It is not for them to understand. You must continue. In these moments, you in all your fierceness must stand alone, completely unapologetic in the path you believe to be true. Some situations that magically find their way to your doorstep will be supplied with supporters as well as detractors. Hold firm to your True North. Here's the funny thing—after some milestone accomplishment, those same people may come to you and offer congratulations. They may even sprinkle in their 20/20 hindsight or back-handed compliment, suggesting they knew you had it in you all the time. That's why at the end of the day you need to keep going, no matter what the cost. If you believe in the direction you are being called to follow, and it is selfless, carefully planned, and most importantly, of value to others—don't stop. Just keep moving forward. Looking back is a distraction that sometimes masks itself in doubt and fear. These distractions are not your friends. Unfortunately, they are masterfully woven into our DNA, and sometimes we must be reminded by others sent into our lives at the appointed time that we are the masters of our fate. Remember, you are fearfully and wonderfully made. Act like it.

I transitioned from field services into the service desk. This was a ridiculously unconventional move thirty years ago! No one in their right mind would have done such a thing. I remember spending the first couple of weeks repeatedly explaining the move to other colleagues. Over and over again, people wanted to understand the why. They just couldn't believe I would consciously do such a thing.

Moving from a field services technical-engineering-type role into the service desk was a transition that I enjoyed immensely. Understanding the origin of the requests we used to receive on our beepers—yeah, those things gave a completely different perspective and appreciation for what the service desk team handled every single day. They took all the crap. Truth be told, more than thirty years later, the IT service desk in just about every organization across the world has experienced that "whipping boy" treatment by their customers that cannot be ignored. They were and remain the underbelly of the IT organization—the duck feet moving at a hundred miles per hour under the surface trying to make sense of a barrage of upset customers, malfunctioning infrastructure, technical know-how that seem simple to the IT-initiated but complex to the lay person. The service desk, regardless of its organization and location, is an easy target and lightning rod for accountability-free criticism that most people and other IT professionals never experience. They are the front-facing portal to the customer's interaction with IT. They are as effective as the support given to them by their leadership and technical partners.

Just so we are crystal clear, the service desks that I've had the pleasure to work with were outstanding. In my experience, if you staff a service desk with exceptionally talented analysts, network technicians, server engineers, application analysts, and desktop personnel, you can effectively reduce the escalation calls and ticket volume to tier two and tier three support. How do I know this to be true? Because of the number of customer second and third return calls associated with unnecessary escalations that could be substantially reduced with improved knowledge base entries, automated self-service tools, seasoned technical expertise, and a laser focus on continued improvement of technical aptitude and customer service—not simply customer service alone. It is a delicate balance that leaders have today to properly set expectations for service delivery and first tier troubleshooting and blend it with *experienced* analysts—not first-timers attempting to "get into IT" through the back door of the service desk. It is a pervasive theme that many leaders of any service desk, regardless of the location, hear all the time: "The service desk is a great place to get into IT. You can cut your teeth there and then decide which field you ultimately want to venture into." This statement in and of itself is true; what's missing is an understanding of the fine balance between exceptional first call closure and paying for talent. You as a leader would be remiss to shortcut the staff's general level of expertise in order to put a butt in a seat and answer a phone. Don't believe me—go ask the higher-tier senior engineering staff who are inundated with calls that should never reach them. While you're at it, please review the cost-per-call financials of having a tier three engineer resolve an issue versus your tier one and two support or field services professionals. Leveraging talent at the expense of expediency and unwillingness to accept a fundamental truth can be catastrophic to the long-term success of any organization if they fail to pay for and staff for the unforeseen business-critical outages, not the everyday routine operations.

Some days, as you can imagine, were significantly better than others in terms of call volume, rude customers, and enterprise disruptions. Learning to manage back-to-back-to-back calls ranging from a simple password reset to switch configurations or telecommunications changes for an entire department groomed me for what was to follow in the now-familiar realm of IT service management, or what is now known as ITSM. Back then, we just did the work without the pretty name attached to it.

During my ten-year service desk journey, I learned mainframe DB2 administration and principles that exposed me to the world of the information security. For a hot minute, I enjoyed it so much so that I sat for the CISSP exam, in which I came up a little short. It was all part of the journey. What I came to realize about myself was I preferred to work with the people that understood how to execute the technology—not administer the technology. The visceral reaction that comes from being a part of the team that partners with others is still to this day extremely rewarding to me. I understood just enough security back then to be dangerous. My hat is off to the information security professionals in today's world. Jesus! You have to be "on" 24/7/365! Kudos to the many security professionals, network analysts, storage junkies, application nerds, and server professionals we take for granted as we swipe our way, unsuspectingly, through the global cyber-security world of immediate electronic self-gratification. Pockets of our society have become so absorbed by our own self-perceived brilliance and privilege that we have become completely blind to those who remain hungry for what a lot of us take for granted—the basic necessities of life: water, food, shelter, access to quality education, and equal treatment under law. As Americans, we are sometimes spoiled by our own global narcissism. Our pockets of intentional separation through misplaced beliefs of varying degrees of superiority have made us profoundly weaker as a people and a nation. We can do better. We will do better together. Standing on what is right will place you in good company more often than not.

Overall, during this tremendous technical learning period I would also gain experience in a variety of disciplines: service management, service recovery, and customer relationship management. I had access to the complete customer lifecycle. I made plenty of mistakes during my immersion. Thankfully, I had genuine, caring leadership that understood the people side just as much the technical side of IT.

Which brings me to our next leadership point. You never know where your next great mentor is going to come from. During my tutelage into what caring leadership looked like from my lens, Tommy T. was an excellent service desk manager and telecommunications professional. If I had to describe Tommy in one word, it would be "unflappable." He was cool as a cucumber. I loved that about him. Easy-going, intellectually astute about his telecommunications and IT business, Tommy was a younger version of Steve and our "grandpa" of the group—because he was a bit older, but also because of his extensive years of experience in the IT industry. Steve even called Tommy "young fella" as well. It was Steve's way of letting us young guys know he still had a few tricks up his sleeve that we didn't know about. Even when I had the rare occasion to witness Tommy get upset, his voice barely rose above a whisper. Nothing ever seemed to rattle him into unprofessionalism. Tommy was also an effective collaborator and bridge builder: poised, professional, and committed to helping the service desk team as well as the other IT teams win every single day. He covered us when we needed protection, inspired us when needed encouragement, and got in our ear when we needed to move with a greater sense of urgency. Tommy was the kind of leader for whom I would have run through a brick wall without a helmet. Great leadership does that *for* you. Great leadership also does that *to* you.

Leadership Lesson Thirteen: During what may seem like complete chaos, do not panic and react. Slow down, ask meaningful questions, and respond appropriately.

Experienced leaders crave information in the midst of a storm—not speculation, gossip, unverified hyperbole, or anecdotes. I remember emphasizing to our service desk teams during my tenure as their leader, "When the world speeds up, we slow down." Tommy was paramount in teaching me the value of poise during chaos in my service desk journey, which I ultimately added to my budding "management-in-training" toolkit.

I would be completely remiss if I didn't mention one of my favorite IT people ever—Tommy Trexler's wife, Ginny T. Being a movie junky, I love a great story. The blockbuster movie *Forrest Gump* is a classic and one of my favorites, if you haven't guessed. You already know where I'm going. She would smile and laugh every time she saw me coming. I would do my best impersonation of Forrest Gump (Tom Hanks), and Ginny would humor me with a laugh. She was also in the telecommunications space at that time, and she was a sharp cookie who was also very genuine in her desire to help others. That kind soul is what I liked about Ginny. You never felt like your presence was a bother to her. She and Tommy both possessed the skill to make people feel at ease. They will forever have my respect. I miss working with both of them. We all love working with and around people who channel positive energy tempered in kindness.

Navigating the world of service delivery into a management position, where I was responsible for others' professional growth and development, continues to be a humbling service endeavor that I will not ever take for granted. Nothing puts the modest success I've been blessed with in better perspective like when I reflect on the many professionals who have come through the service desk on their way to bigger, better opportunities that were discovered, nurtured with the tools shared with me by the many leaders who invested in my success. They gave of themselves unselfishly. They didn't use people as disposable chess pieces for their own personal gain or professional advancement. These leaders understood that service to others would ultimately prevail. Their willingness to serve others, uprightness of character, and solid value system proved to be a winning combination every single time. These leaders gave me something to aspire to. I wanted to do and be better.

Chapter Thirteen

When I think of bow ties and my first indoctrination into the accessory that would forever capture the essence of my personal style, the first image that comes to mind is that Marriott lobby photo of the father and son—the same picture that popped into my head the moment I saw Dick and Chester in the office preparing to greet me for my interview. They both looked as smooth as a Brooks Brothers' ad. Classic business jackets, artful but not overly stated suspenders (real ones, with the buttons inside the pants), crisply pressed shirts with subtle cufflinks . . . and elegant bow ties. On the side table, I noticed a nice fedora, which I suspected was Dick's because we were in his office, and I remember him being a fedora guy—Chester, not so much. Although I was young and very impressionable at the time, I kept thinking in that moment everything about those two spoke "class" to me. I was instantly impressed with these two gentlemen. The funny thing was, I remember being completely at ease and not one bit nervous. To my surprise, I was unusually calm. I have no recollection of what we talked about at all. What I do remember with exacting clarity was what happened immediately after the interview was over.

I don't remember the man's real name, but I will forever call him "Mr. Magoo"—you know, the cartoon character—because he was an elderly, small-statured, well-dressed gentleman. He walked with a slow, unforgettably bent over walk. And he forever changed my fashion life.

Upon leaving the interview with Dick and Chester, I was, of course, excited about how the interview had seemed to go well. However, what I was most looking forward to was heading to the mall and learning how to tie a real bow tie. Nothing was going to get in my way as I anxiously raced to the mall to see my mission through. There is where I first laid eyes on Mr. Magoo.

As I raced into the store, Mr. Magoo stood behind the counter, bent over, folding some shirts. He looked up at me, pleasantly curious.

I was very clear in my expectations. "Sir, I want to learn how to tie a real bow tie, and I'm not leaving here until you show me! I don't want any clip-ons. I want a real bow tie."

Mr. Magoo, seeing my enthusiasm and failing to be impressed, looked up from his current task spoke calmly. "Sonny, grab two of those ties right there, and meet me over at that mirror."

It felt like it took him three days to get over to that full-length mirror, taking his Mr. Magoo mini steps, but he eventually made it. My excitement was not dashed in the least. I waited patiently while I marveled at his speed.

He was a gem.

As we stood side by side in front of that mirror, Mr. Magoo masterfully demonstrated in just under two minutes how to successfully tie a bow tie. My first attempt actually turned out pretty darn good. A bit clumsy, but still not bad for my initial foray into this new fashion world, with which I was completely unfamiliar. Now I was really on fire with excitement! Standing in front of that mirror with a relatively well-done bow tie, I felt very proud. I felt like the slick-looking interviewers I'd left just an hour earlier. I felt as if I belonged. I was twenty-three years old and did not understand that I really didn't know squat about the realities of the professional world. I was green as green could be. I was just an excited kid longing to become a part of something new; something bigger than anything I could become alone; something real that meant I now had a place in this world.

Mr. Magoo, seeing my prideful excitement, directed me to the bow tie rack and informed me to buy only thin, silk bow ties. He explained that when you are first starting out, they are a bit easier to tie than thicker cloth bow ties. I heard him, but I was not listening. He set me straight at checkout. He helped me select five really nice bow ties. It was probably three too many, but I didn't care. I was now officially in the club. Clip-ons, kick rocks . . . forever!

Now, here's the part of the story that to this day remains an endearing memory. Handing me the nicely wrapped bow ties I had just paid for in a rather sophisticated bag, Mr. Magoo leaned over the counter and said, "Sonny, now let me tell you what's going to happen to you when you go to tie those bow ties. You're gonna sweat like a pig, and your forearms are gonna burn like fire!"

Not only was I completely and utterly confused by his statement I was so ready to get out of there and head home, but his final message stopped me in my tracks. I did not understand what in the hell Mr. Magoo was talking about. He didn't explain it. I was so excited with what I'd just learned that it didn't matter. I had my bow ties in hand, and I was ready to just get out of there and head home with my new and classy accessories. Mr. Magoo looked at me with a wry smile and sent me on my way. My confusion and short-lived agitation with my instructor's final message to me was quickly replaced by my newfound skill of elite fashion etiquette.

Fast-forward to about four months later. A benefit dinner provided me with the perfect opportunity to wear one of my bow ties. Although it had been a while since my initial introduction into the bow tie fashion elite, my enthusiasm was now higher than ever. I pressed and starched a white dress shirt for the event. Next, I eagerly proceeded to begin tying the bow tie according to Mr. Magoo's instructions. I quickly realized that my arms were in an uncomfortably raised position, and I suffered an unanticipated lack of dexterity in my fingers now that I didn't have the immediate counsel of Mr. Magoo, bow tie savant. As I determinedly pressed forward, I repeatedly fumbled with the knot, failing to arrange the bow tie using the same method I'd learned in the store just four months earlier. My several unsuccessful attempts took what felt like forever. My family was calling for me to hurry up. Their pressure fostered a rising frustration that eventually turned into fury after almost an hour of this so-called labor of love.

My family made one last desperate request that I hurry up and get downstairs. I remember my outburst as if it was ten seconds ago: "I'm coming! I can't get this damn bow tie!" Then it hit me. My crisp white shirt was completely soaked, I was sweating like a pig, and my forearms were on fire! I stood there looking in the mirror in total disbelief and utter amazement at not only my complete ineptitude, but also the realization that Mr. Magoo's message was as prophetically accurate as they come. That smug, tiny son of a you-know-what! I could only laugh out loud at myself, change my shirt, and try again.

Eventually, I was able to get the bow tie tied well enough to be appropriate for the evening. I've been wearing them ever since. That is how the bow tie has forever made its way into my wardrobe and my heart.

The other part about the bowtie that I enjoy, if I'm being completely honest, is that the bow tie accessory is simply not for everyone. Anyone can wear one, but that doesn't mean they should. People realize quickly if the bow tie is something they should add to their wardrobe or not. This is partly why I'm drawn to them—you create your style by choosing your colors, your flavor. You make them your own. The bow tie would become one of my calling cards. Service to people would be the other.

The growth of my bow tie collection has been more than thirty years in the making. It's still growing. Most of the time, a bow tie is a completely spontaneous purchase that sneaks up on me without warning. I could be looking for something else or nothing at all, and then all of a sudden—*bam!* There it is, calling me. "Hey you—psst—yeah, you. Get over here and check me out. You don't have this style in your closet. Take me home. No need to get two or three today. Just one. Me. I'm the only one you need."

Sometimes, however, I go purposefully looking for a specific pattern or color, and that is when I struggle to find bow ties that speak to me. So now, I've learned to just let them appear however they see fit. From there, I will decide if that little voice in my head gets listened to or not.

Being introduced to the new world of healthcare IT continues to be an exciting exercise in learning. I love the collective brain trust of an urban university, academic medical center, and IT organization all operating in the same sphere of serving the public health and scholarly excellence simultaneously. These employees show up every day and consistently make the exceptional look routine. They are the true heroes. I was an IT cog that occasionally stepped out from behind the curtain entrusted with outstanding people to carry out the mission of providing an exceptional user experience for patients through technology. Failure to execute clinical excellence is not an option for these warriors. Having to make life and death medical decisions with incredible poise is also not for the faint of heart. Working in IT in a complex academic medical center, one thing became clear very quickly to me—people die if critical applications malfunction. These critical services all operate in an intricate collaboration focused on one objective: providing reliable and secure IT services for thousands of clinicians so they can provide exceptional patient care, period. I had been well prepared for this job of life and death. Service to others in the midst of the sometimes cruel realities of life itself positioned me well to handle this new role in one of the premier academic medical centers in the country. Tutelage from others laid the foundation of concrete slabs called perseverance and resolve that supported me. They would serve me well in this new journey of discovery that was healthcare information technology.

My first adventure in the world of healthcare IT came in the form of an introduction inside a dungeon—or at least, that's what I called it. The room where I met my new team was a nasty-looking room filled with papers, dusty boxes, and tiny cubicles shared by team members in the basement of the hospital, which was called the CSC. I called the room a dungeon because that was the first word that came to mind when I saw it. Unwelcoming, dark, dirty, and small. A dungeon.

I fondly remember the look I got from one of the veteran service desk staff members, Ms. Shirley B. It was a classic moment that I smile to reflect on, knowing now what would transpire during our five years together. It was that look that all of us have received at one time or another from a family member, friend, or parent. The look said, "Boy, don't come in here thinking you're about to change anything! We don't know you, and we ain't studdin' you!" For those of you who are unfamiliar with the word "studdin'," let me be crystal clear—I made it up, but most of you know exactly what I just said. "We don't give a damn about what you think you're going to try and do up in here! We are not paying attention to or remotely interested in what you're talking about!" Add a scowl and a furrowed brow, and there you have it. The look that said it all. In today's vernacular, it would go something like this, "Boy, bye!" That cold greeting would eventually be replaced with mutual respect, fierce loyalty (Ms. Shirley wouldn't let anyone mess with me), and professionalism that I would hold close during my steep learning curve.

Ms. Shirley was a warrior. She was this itty-bitty thing who lived big. Although the last of her multiple battles with breast cancer took her from us at the young age of fifty-five, Ms. Shirley would leave an indelible, positive, and loving mark on my soul forever. She was my first healthcare IT angel, and she kept me out of harm's way as this new journey unfolded.

Leadership Lesson Fourteen: Say what you mean and mean what you say.

What I loved most about Ms. Shirley was that she taught me that lesson. Ms. Shirley taught me the lesson to let your yes be yes, and let your no be no. Don't mince words. Be plain. Do not be rude. Be clear. Own it. I loved Ms. Shirley. I would come to benefit from yet another titan of a leader—also named Shirley—who would nurture my career well beyond any leader's responsibilities. There is no doubt about it. I have been truly blessed way beyond what I deserve.

So have you.

Leadership is a perpetual lesson in humility. It requires constant attention to detail, persistent work toward the common goal, and an insatiable appetite for improvement. The areas that are most exposed to others that we attempt to keep hidden because we believe they are weaknesses (fears, doubts, and insecurities) often require the most effort to develop. These are sometimes the weaknesses we ignore the most. Not because they are difficult, but because we believe that they are impossible to correct. We can be our own worst enemy at times. This new service desk group required from me a skillset that I had not used in quite some time. These skills had been almost completely sucked out of me by my previous employer. These skills were now layered with intense frustration. Care was her name. Love would be her companion. This opportunity allowed an important distraction: someone needed to pour into them. Someone needed to love and care for them. This new group had not seen either in a very long time. Some of the best advice ever given to me was when you're coming out of a storm, try focusing more on others and less on yourself. Recalling this advice years later was appropriate with this new group of professionals. It was a mutually beneficial relationship.

One word immediately came to mind when I saw this location and team—neglect. This group of professionals were clearly working their tails off and had not been treated with decency and respect for a very long time. They had been relegated to the dungeon, left to fend for themselves with minimal supervision and paltry resources. This was not acceptable. The moment my director left me alone with them, they proceeded to unload all their complaints upon me quickly and without warning. They were capable and competent but professionally malnourished.

I fondly remember that, on my first day experiencing this new team and its challenging location in November of 2008, I was also introduced to their version of an enterprise outage board. This was classic. It was an uneven, poorly set up white tripod sitting in the middle of the floor, with a dirty whiteboard and half-erased words in colored markers that were barely legible. I couldn't believe it. There I was, standing in the middle of this dirty and quite dusty sham of an office space that was clearly too small in a prominent academic medical center, and this was the best this team was given? This was a level-one, nationally recognized trauma center and at that time a two-billion-dollar organization at the time. And a dirty white board was the best they could do for the service desk? Hell no. All the low-hanging fruit became quickly apparent with this assignment. I was very excited to be a part of this team.

The two-on-one drill from my basketball days was determined to make a cameo at my new job. This time it was the organization and the outside world against this new service desk. We had little moral support; meager resources; and a few burned-out, openly apathetic team members not interested in improving anything. Mediocrity had crept into their DNA and become the new normal. There were a few dedicated team members; it only takes one, but we had four specifically who wanted better. They became the bedrock we needed to move the service desk needle forward. These new responsibilities made us feel like it was us against the world. These odds were once again not in our favor. Bad odds were my favorite. It's not difficult to smile when good odds are on the table easily accessible to you. Anyone can cheer for good odds. That is easy. Getting excited about odds not in your favor when the world says, "This group? You mean the 'helpless desk'? What can they do for us?" Yes, I like proving people wrong. More importantly, I love seeing people who have been minimized and discounted by others elevate their professional and personal performance in the midst of nay-sayers. Even if the things I told myself in order to find the motivation to carry on did not in turn motivate others, it was the self-imposed fuel to feed my mission—to serve others. To be of value to others and make a difference that impacts them positively. It was this purpose that I've instinctively gravitated to my entire life in order to manufacture and maintain the momentum that both progress and meaningful change demand.

I needed to find love and caring quickly. Truth be told, I needed this group more than they needed me as their leader. But really, we both needed each other. There are no coincidences. My being maneuvered there was purposeful, even if I couldn't see it at the time.

Chapter Fourteen

Sometimes being responsible for others is simply no fun at all. Carrying that bucket of responsibility for performance, professional direction, morale, results, and your own sanity can be daunting at times. How do you manage it? How do you successfully navigate the often-ridiculous demands of leadership while sustaining the illusion that you can do it all?

If you're smart, you quickly realize you can't do it all. That very notion that you can will lead you down a path destined for failure. This path is riddled with landmines of self-criticism, accolades, misplaced ambition, temporary success, and unforeseen failures all wrapped in the relentlessly unforgiving expectations of others who have no idea who you really are and why you're really here. It's interesting, really, how it all manifests itself. Often the illusion appears as carefully crafted "succession planning" or career coaching. It's all designed to make us believe that we can do it all. We can be all things to everyone, all the time. Leadership unmasked as if it were a mystery. Leadership is not complicated to understand. It simply takes courage and a discerning spirit to execute it. Others may call it emotional intelligence. Label it as you wish. What's important is that we all get to understand when a moment requires is a contribution from us and when it does not. We know right and wrong when we experience them. Understand this: you cannot do it all. The sooner you realize that, the sooner you can move closer to your purpose.

My wife, Cynthia, calls it "believing your own hype." She's so much smarter than I am. She's actually a Marvel Comics superhero masquerading as my wife, but she pulls off the "mere mortal" routine with flawless precision. The hype says, "Look at me! Look at how successful I am. You can do it too! Just follow my lead. Better yet: read my book, like my Instagram post, follow me on Twitter." In the immortal words of one of my favorite TV personalities, Michael Wilbon from ESPN's *Pardon the Interruption*, "Shut UP!" Enough already. Since we can't have peas without carrots, I must also give a shoutout to the other half of that Emmy-award winning duo, Tony Kornheiser. They are my entertaining and extremely talented sports journalism slice of heaven with a dash of mancave bravado mixed with a better research team than Google analytics sprinkled in for good measure. I love these guys. They are literary and consummate professionals each in their own right, and together they are magic.

As for my wife—yeah, she is a genius, and I married up.

Technology has made our world so much smaller. The birth of social media has created a transparency never before seen in the history of civilization. It is an amazing and fantastic achievement that we all can responsibly participate in. Sometimes however, we should just keep some things to ourselves.

Every day, we witness another casualty of social media. Some of these are innocent, while others are completely self-inflicted. I really wish everyone would stop for a second to think before hitting "send" on a post. The vastness of the internet and immediacy of posting there can be overwhelming. You can tweet it, Snap it, Facebook it, Pinterest it, post it, live stream it, Facebook Live it, and on and on. The need to be liked by masses of followers has not only replaced our intrinsic desire for self-fulfilling progress; it has completely stifled our ability to manage meaningful real-life relationships with one another.

Let me be clear: I understand that social media has generally been a wonderful advancement in our ability to communicate globally and access a variety of people, talent, and resources with astonishing speed. The creation and global proliferation of social media continues to be one of the world's greatest achievements in human capitalism and creative ingenuity.

As a leader, you must choose your battles wisely. What requires your immediate attention? Is it process, people, or technology? There may be some healthy debate on this one. Healthy debate is a good thing. Multiple perspectives are a good thing. Apathy, on the other hand, is not good. Use your voice boldly and confidently. Mean what you say and say exactly what you mean.

I belong to the leadership school of thought that chooses people first every single time. Looking back on my initial IT career, I realize I had two men who took a chance on me, an unknown entity with zero telecommunications experience and even less real-world work experience. They picked people first. Address the people first, and you will more than likely head in the right direction. People are my mission. It is through the people that the mission is accomplished. As a leader, your job isn't to fix anyone.

Hell, you and I are broken ourselves. Truth be told, we all wear a mask. We all are broken. Channeling creative energy through our talents can mend us. Each of us have unique gifts. We would be doing others a tremendous disservice by not exploring, developing, and sharing those abilities with the world for the benefit of others. People are my first choice. People matter. People make the difference.

Whichever you decide—people, process, or technology—prioritize what is important to you in your individual leadership journey. Believing that all three can be equally balanced is not practical in its application, nor is it realistic in its execution. Technology is moving at lightspeed while the demands on people's time exponentially increases, requiring us to be more efficient and process-oriented in how we manage that time. People, processes, and technologies are not made equal. You should be committed and enthusiastic about your outcomes. As leaders, we all want that elusive balance to have and do it all. The prioritizing of one is not the exclusion of the others, but a purposeful decision to trust your leadership style and honor it. Remember, we can't do all, but we can have it all—just not at the same time. Really inspiring leaders have vision, passion, and decisive direction. There is absolutely nothing worse than an indecisive leader being responsible for a lot of things on the boardroom table.

You know what? I take that back. There is something worse: a timid leader who becomes manipulated into doing another's bidding. *That* leader is far worse. Because that leader doesn't have the courage to pivot when required, they become victim to the strong, those who are better equipped to maneuver the obstacles and do the heavy lifting when necessary. Strength is not always right. Allowing yourself to become a morally bankrupt leader swayed by the dubious scruples of another is the epitome of leadership betrayal.

Looking around at the environment and attitude of this service desk group, it became apparent that this new team needed reinforcement that what they did every single day mattered. The complacency of a mundane and under-appreciated routine clung to them like a mothy sweater in desperate need of a local dry cleaner, so familiar that you don't even realize it smells because you wear it every day. This stinky routine had become their new normal.

As a leader, one of your primary objectives is to instill unwavering confidence in your people. You can demonstrate this through behaviors that support the mission of the organization. You can't always perfectly align your value system, your team's, the department's, or even the organization's with the company's, though it's a wonderful coincidence when that happens. As the honcho, you will be called on to make decisions about whether something should proceed because it is in the department's best interest even when it may be a low priority on the "big board" of the organization. This does not mean you and your team are operating outside the bounds of the organization; it simply means actions will occasionally be different from strategic objectives. These tactics may not align at all levels. Some of your staff may share values with the company or with each other. That is normal. Some of your staff will have different value systems from yours. This is also normal. When your values as the leader differ to such a degree that the outward expression of those values manifest themselves inappropriately to the detriment of the team—that's when you address it in order to right the ship and maintain your strategic course. Your success as a leader depends on it. Failure to act now, hoping that someone or something will change on its own, is simply wishful thinking.

How do you get to even understand your team's value system and its importance to them? You meet with your team and listen to them. They will tell you everything that's going on. If you listen long enough to hear what it is, they have to say. Remember that occasionally finding out a person's "why" is more important than directing them get something done. Command and control or parent-child management strategies are not efficient long-term strategies for continued organizational improvement. Others more intelligent than I have spent their entire lives studying organizational management theories that have withstood the tests of time and scrutiny, so I will not belabor the point. People are complex beings; yet they all share the simple desire to be valued and respected rather than simply being told what to do and how to do it. Now, it's important to note here that effective teams are also built on fundamental respect for the positions of authority that our leaders occupy. Leaders should absolutely be given the respect of their position, and sometimes when the leader says, "Here's what we're going to do . . ." that is the essence and end of the conversation. Get it done, and keep the train moving.

During my first two weeks on the job, I met with every member of the team. Getting a sense of their "why," how they believed they were being treated, what mattered to them, and what they thought of the "new guy" was time well spent. A key takeaway from those one-on-one meetings was that people simply want to be heard. They want to be listened to and valued. Some of them had quite frankly already checked out.

Some were glad I was there. Others could have cared less that I was the new dude sent to develop the team into a cohesive unit, create a culture of accountability, streamline processes, and improve the reputation of a team that had become accustomed to mediocrity. I was just a dude who had been uprooted and planted in new soil, and I was now in desperate need of cultivation. This dungeon in the bowels of the hospital was not suited to building a team capable of so much more—dark, cramped, and dirty, without care or concern about what was going on outside of its boundaries. We had more room in the bathroom across the hall. I knew I had to pick my battles: the dysfunctional team, terrible work conditions, poor morale, or the lack of processes. There was plenty to choose from.

As I mentioned earlier, wearing the mantle of leadership can sometimes be exhausting. It can also be quite exhilarating when done intentionally.

After meeting with everyone, it was apparent that a couple battles were more pressing than others. "Battle" is actually not the right term here because it implies confrontation. No, I had been trained to be a strategic thinker, so I knew very early on that I needed some help. I quickly learned where human resources lived. Some of the best advice I ever received was a golden nugget from a former VP: "HR are like the police. They are your friends. Go make nice well before you need them. Be nice when interacting with them, because you will see them again. Make plenty of deposits. Get to know them. Allow them to get to know you.

If you head down this management trail, you will make some withdrawals. You will need the support of human resources well before they need you."

I would realize later what the VP was trying to teach me. He was helping me understand the value of building quality relationships. I made several purposeful "drive-bys" during my first months on the job. This was solid advice then, and it's even more solid now as the years slip beyond our once youthful inexperience, when we believed we had all the answers. We don't. Some learn this valuable lesson early on. The key is having way more deposits stored up than withdrawals. HR can make your life a living nightmare, or it can be a safe haven. I chose to make it the latter. Once again, the people in HR made all the difference. They are still some of my greatest heroes and most valued colleagues.

HR wasn't my only stop. I made several important rounds during those first few months getting to know the landscape. Remember, I knew squat about healthcare. I sometimes just walked around from one department to the next, getting to know the department heads, nurse managers, and everyday team members committed to the common good of the organization.

One sidebar worth mentioning here is that the doctors get the all the glory, but make no mistake about it—nurses run the show in most if not all hospitals! I learned that important truth within the first few weeks and meetings on the job. The quote, from a prominent male surgeon, went something like this, "HH, I know I can be a bit of prima donna with my demands and all, but here's the deal: the tail that wags the dog here are our nurses! They know their stuff. Do not ever forget that." That paint stroke of advice stuck immediately and never dripped from the canvas of my experience. This provider, who shall forever remain nameless, was a royal thorn in my side during my first year, but they soon thereafter became one of our most loyal supporters and an advocate for the service desk. The conflict during our first year was definitely one of the most beneficial times in my young healthcare IT career. Battling against perception, speaking to new ways of working, and shifting a cultural paradigm sometimes unwilling to be moved consistently placed me in harm's way. More often than not, however, we begin winning hearts and minds through solid service and realistic expectations built on one brick of credibility at a time.

As we discussed previously: All conflict is not bad. Sometimes it's just plain necessary.

Chapter Fifteen

Relationships. We are built for them. Some seek them out. Some avoid them at all costs. We nurture them and we destroy them. That magic thread of genuinely caring for another person's well-being that ties the impersonal to the doable. Relationships have the potential to turn the seemingly insignificant into awesome accomplishments when people choose to work together for good of the team and not their ego. As I've mentioned, I prefer to address the people issues first. They are the root of the dysfunction you as the leader seek to conquer. They are also the perpetual thorns in your side that will not go away, even if you choose to ignore them.

Understanding what needed to be said was critical during the early stages of our new team's development. Remember: listen first, process second, and comment third. My trusted bow ties would be a huge icebreaker for some. For others, a polite entry into surface conversations would ultimately grow into long-lasting, healthy business and personal connections. Identifying the keepers on this service desk team was secondary to finding those who did not want to be there and "encouraging" them to find their happiness elsewhere. Disgruntled, unhappy, complacent, disrespected, non-enthusiastic employees are a slow, crippling toxin that kills from within. Dispassionate employees methodically extract the lifeblood of good will, focused intention, pride, and professionalism out of every good-intentioned team member. Their unprofessional attitudes and passive-aggressive remarks about strategic direction made it very clear that they were no longer committed to the cause. Here's the funny thing: As I look back on those early days, most of the "haters" not sold on this new team were folks who didn't care for the bow tie. Weird, right? How could this possibly be a mere coincidence? It was peculiar as all get out. I didn't let this bother me. I stayed focused on the task at hand—keep and develop team members committed to improving. Period.

Don't overcomplicate your mission. We do this often, in part by adding stuff into the mix that doesn't need to be there. As leaders, we are ultimately responsible for the teams we manage, as well as the outcomes. You better be able to look yourself in the mirror when the rubber meets the road. What do I mean? You must create an environment for all team members to win first. Part of leading is nurturing; part of nurturing is coaching. Part of coaching is intentional and candid dialogue without the BS. Get to it. Positive momentum, progress, and a staff that will consistently stretch themselves toward greatness will be its own reward.

We immediately set out to create boundaries for the team based on feedback from the everyone and my overall experience dealing with multi-functional service desk personnel. Now, we were getting somewhere. Over the next several months, the herd separated quickly into three distinct camps: believers, non-believers, and whiners.

The believers were just that—believers. They got it right away. They understood what we were changing and what needed to be done differently with this service desk team. They knew that accountability was being introduced, and it was not going to be ignored. This group constituted the part of the team that understood the complexity of the medical center far better than I did. They had made a conscious decision to work with me for the greater good of the organization. I really appreciated that effort in the early stages of our working relationship. These true professionals carried me when I had no clue about the intricacies of such a complex academic medical center.

The next group, the non-believers, were polite yet unconvinced that this new "flavor of the month" leader was worth their time and emotional investment. Ms. Shirley and a couple others fell into this category. They needed more time. More time for me to say something contradictory. More time for my actions to not line up with my words. More time to either solidify their initial visceral reaction or change course with the ammunition provided by my own mismanaged decisions. They kept waiting. It would take some time, but in just under a year, this group would come on board and help steady the ship that was leaving the port of mediocrity. This initial group of non-believers would be by far the most important group. These four service desk staffers (Shirley B., Mike E., Cleo C., and Valerie W.) would fight for me, stand alongside me, and remain immovable through thick and thin. These four trusted and extremely competent professionals steadied the ship during the storms of change and transition to leaner, faster, smarter, and better. Of this initial group of four, only one remains. Her place is forever sealed in my heart as a trusted colleague and friend. She knows who she is. Thank you for your loyalty and leadership, Valerie W.—even when you absolutely didn't feel like leading.

Now, to the whiners. Every organization has them. Although there were not many of them, they enthusiastically constituted the bulk of the noise for the team. A couple of these folks were clearly disgruntled about their standing, while others were flat-out pissed that the service desk manager's job did not come their way. One very vocal woman was by far the best qualified to lead the group. It really wasn't even close. I should have just packed up my number two pencil, all three of my slick little bowties, and called it a career. Why was I even there? Oh, I remember now, it was because nobody liked her, including my director at the time. My director made it very clear that the disgruntled team member would not be a good fit for this role. It happens. Maybe you have experienced the disappointment of not being selected for a role that you believed you were more than qualified for. Perhaps you were absolutely correct, but the "fit" wasn't good for the person making the hiring decision. Yeah, it does happen. Accept the reality, and keep it moving.

Building a new team often requires the removal of some old, crumbling foundation that must be replaced with more solid footing to ensure stability during the rebuilding process. In my mentoring sessions with team members, I would use the "bricks of credibility" metaphor to train them in a thought process that would build a stronger service desk, one brick at a time. These bricks were phone calls, walk-ins, electronic web submittals, and other customer interactions. By getting the team to focus on small and consistent successes, we could win big together. We could shore up the new foundation with solidly constructed interactions that strengthened our collective team in addition to improving the overall perception of the service desk in the eyes of our customers and IT. The whiners were not having any of it. My every recommendation felt like tug-of-war. It quickly became exhausting. When I asked questions, they were met with disgust disguised as playful sarcasm. Classic passive-aggressive behavior was on full display for all to see. It would only get worse. My actions and experiences were supposed to give each team member the opportunity to change work situations for the better and implement recommendations they believed would propel the team forward, but all I got in return was a blatantly casual work ethic dripping with resentment. They were testing their boundaries with me to see how much they could get away with, how much would I ignore in an effort to preserve the peace. New leaders are quite familiar with this interesting dynamic. This is a crucial moment for leaders, which can positively impact the culture of the team far beyond the current moment, and it must be dealt with immediately. You as leader must respond. The question is, how? It is time to encourage some team members to find their happiness elsewhere.

Most employees are keenly aware of the how much of a pain it is to properly "manage out"' employees. You must dot your Is and cross your Ts within the human resources process. Due process reigns supreme. Documentation is critical. Some leaders will do anything to avoid additional paperwork. It's labor-intensive and exacting, and it requires an intense focus that a lot of team members bet their leader will simply not have the discipline to complete. Excellent leaders realize what needs to be done, and they do it, even when it's uncomfortable. Complete fairness and objectivity are required. Remember, you want folks to win, but at some point, trying to manage around poor behavior, mediocre performance, and a lack of accountability becomes a tremendous drain on the entire team. If the complete lack of accountability is left unresolved for the not-so-happy sailors, your entire ship will sink—and so will you as their leader.

After some employees decided that this new service desk was not going to be part of their future, they left the team, and we began a journey of discovery that led to our hiring and developing a ton of talented new rock stars. A lot of these initial new service desk personnel have moved on to different departments and disciplines inside as well as outside of the organization. We have former service desk team members who work in application support, desktop services, network, virtual and physical servers, mobility services, virtual desktop infrastructure for remote support—and all of them were once led by a guy who continues helping others find their way to what was already theirs to claim in the first place. They just needed an encouraging nudge in the right direction. Sometimes, even unbeknownst to them, due to the chaos, the lies and confusion of everyday life and the constant barrage of excessive stimuli that stealthily covers them until they cannot even see through the fog of the misdirection that so easily distracts them from their true purpose. As leaders, it is our responsibility to help those in our care by unveiling their true gifts and talents that may not be readily apparent, not hold them hostage to the antiquated model of parent-child management devoid of compassion and genuine concern to better the human condition.

Our leadership journey will inevitably bring us to the doorstep of legacy. Be very careful here. This threshold has tripped up some of the best leaders. There is a direct correlation between the ego-seeking knucklehead not paying attention to the signals and the unfortunate outcomes that make great companies good, good companies mediocre, and mediocre companies file for bankruptcy. Some leaders drive right pass these important, yet often subtle signs (poor morale, consistently apathetic behaviors, missed assignments with zero consequences, and the occasional "I'm not sure about that but I will find out," which can also serve as a placeholder to the proverbial "whatever") because "I want to make sure I leave a legacy." If this statement wasn't so dangerous, it would almost be laughable.

How does wanting to leave a genuine legacy of accomplishment differ from the ego-driven leader? The latter expressly makes the journey all about themselves. It is never about anyone or anything else. It most certainly isn't about helping others become successful. Legacy sometimes gets confused with license to intentionally ignore of the needs of others, but not at the cost of the leader. As I've stated before, everyone else gets clipped first; it's never the leader who gets hurt initially. The people who do the heavy lifting are often left to figure out what the intent was because the leader failed to communicate their expectations. The leader steps across all of the professional carnage of mismanaged careers for the express purpose of their own selfish interpretation of what they believe. The uninspired superstars once filled with passion and purpose scattered about the corporate hallways of ambition and promise wondering, "What's going on here? How did this once-excited group of exceptional professionals get here?" Really? The misguided and sometimes insatiable desire to leave a lasting legacy can blind a leader to the business realities happening around them if they stay focused on themselves to the exclusion of all else.

We all know that it's not the pursuit of legacy that is the blind spot; it's the ego and pride attached this pursuit. A savvy leader sees the tripwire. Their lens has a much sharper view due to an acute understanding that it is not about them. They also travel in the consistent safety nets that humility of purpose provides. These folks want to leave something in better shape than they found it, but not at the expense of others' careers and aspirations.

In all my years of serving in a management capacity, I have not experienced a greater feeling of satisfaction than having former employees visit to reminisce with the team and chat about how much gratitude they have for our unwavering support of their dreams and goals during their time on our team. Nothing gets better than that. I get goosebumps when I get that kind of feedback from team members. Knowing that I made a difference in the lives of others is awesome. Your money is no good here. You can't buy your way to the protected safety of your team's genuine desire to succeed, not just for themselves but because they don't want to disappoint you. They want to cover you with not only their competence but also with their compassion. Respect and trust are the currencies that rarely depreciate. It's true that all of it can be mismanaged and even betrayed, but the value of those precious commodities cannot be overstated.

Leadership Lesson Fifteen: The currencies of respect and influence exist as a powerful tandem that should not be casually dismissed.

As I began building relationships with team members from all departments, it became increasingly apparent to me that I had much to learn. I remember sitting in meeting and not having a clue about the medical jargon and acronyms being tossed around. It was as if a completely different language was being spoken, one that everyone in the room understood except me. I would break out my iPad, casually scroll like I was checking something important, and Google the term. That is one method I used to increase my clinical competence. The other was to ask clarifying questions to those I trusted outside of these formal meetings. You know, folks who wouldn't judge me. They wanted to help me learn. I was so green in this new world of healthcare IT, but I was and continue to be fascinated by learning.

As you can imagine, everyone has their detractors. I call them what they really are: player haters. Believe it or not, they are quite necessary in your evolutionary journey. It doesn't matter what your socioeconomic position, organizational status level, or academic achievement level—some people just aren't going to like you. What I've discovered through my mentoring sessions with others more experienced in relationship-building than I is that most of the time it's not actually you or that someone may not like——it's what you represent. Do you represent something they don't like about themselves? Do you have a personality trait they wish they had in their tool bag? Do you hold them accountable where others may not? Do you simply not accept what they say as gospel and challenge their thinking to increase the value of the dialogue?

Famous actor and two-time Academy Award winner Denzel Washington once said, "Your spirit can irritate their demons." Some people will not be inclined to join your team no matter what you attempt to do. Those demons that have never been addressed may inconveniently pop up in your psyche at the most inopportune times to derail your fluid thinking and solid opinion of yourself and others. You've heard it before: "This person has such a warm spirit about them!" Or they have an infectious personality. I bet you can reel off three people you love simply being around because of the positive energy they bring to an environment. You also know another three who force you to quickly and quietly seek the exit sign because of their negative energy that overpowers all in close proximity. I believe there is something to that. Is it their energy, or is it the energy you've attached to them? Those who have simply refused to shift their thinking are resolute in their belief system. They have simply made up their mind about you, and nothing is going to change their minds. You may get a very personal reaction from some in the form of body language, facial expressions, or micro-aggressive comments.

I'm no psychologist, and I don't play one on TV, but I have come to believe in the power of spirits, both good and bad, that are far beyond our naked eye that are as real as the words that you see in front of you. Some may not like how you dress, how you speak, where you went to school, where you are from, your personality—whatever it is, it has nothing to do with you and everything to do with them. Wikipedia defines *psycholog-*

ical projection as "a defense mechanism in which the human ego defends itself against unconscious impulses or qualities by denying their existence in themselves while attributing them to others."

The tendency to find fault in others to mask one's own inadequacies manifests itself long before it shows up in the workplace. Some slight, some deficiency, some trauma created a story that led to a belief, which in turn created an emotion, which led to a behavior that strengthened that core belief or refuted it. Only that person knows what is behind the curtain that they don't want you or anyone to know about, and truth be told, they are never going to tell you about it. Being vulnerable doesn't mean giving your life secrets away, but it does mean being open. Closed-off leadership is leadership stifled, so they will forever be bound by their inability to navigate through an obsolete belief system once thought to be true and move beyond their flawed self-perception in order to not be imprisoned because of it. That is a burden they carry all alone. Their issues are not your problem. Sometimes you have to forbid certain things to penetrate your sacred space. You as the leader don't have to try and save the planet, or even, for that matter, speak on the subject. Let it go and let them deal with it.

Not everyone is going to like you or support your mission. "Get over yourself," as one of my most respected and beloved mentors, Shirley G., would say. Being able to make lemonade from that bag of lemons we are sometimes handed comes with the territory of leadership. Figuring out a way to turn a perceived disappointment or real failure into motivation is a skill that gets sharpened with continued practice.

You and I, however, are headed somewhere. Doubt, fear, and player-haters do not have a seat on this ride. It's our ride; our journey; your purpose; my purpose.

The key is to not grant others permission to bring drama into your space. You have some say in how your energy is going to be use. You just don't have to allow another to consume it with their "hair on fire" rhetoric. This battle that we all are engaged in is not against flesh and blood.

It begins and ends with the mind, which is the ultimate battlefield that will determine our destiny. Those reading this right now who understand what I'm saying may see it very differently from those who don't. This can lead to a healthy debate, inspirational dialogue on things that we cannot see, feel, smell, or touch. Believing in something you cannot see is the embodiment of faith. How can you be sure this is the right decision? What are you willing to risk?

For me, later in my leadership journey, I would literally bet my life on it.

Chapter Sixteen

Early in my management development, I coined the phrase "drive-by" to mean a casual, unplanned visit between colleagues for the purpose of relationship-building with those not in our immediate sphere of influence or workflow. The drive-by caught on quickly. This concept is nothing new, and people have been doing it forever. I am not trying to take credit for an activity that has been around since long before I showed up, but I'll say I had not heard the term being used in any space and at any time in my professional life before I started verbalizing the activity and giving it a formal name. So there. Maybe some lady in Boise, Idaho, coined the phrase at the local diner on Route 17? I don't know. I like the term because it describes an informal, collaborative, light-hearted, and non-threatening visit with a colleague to simply build rapport well before more intense or crucial conversations are held. Having a relationship that is created well before the storm is in direct proportion with how well or how poorly said storm is handled. Again, relationships matter. The drive-by creates and builds trust along with clarifying value systems that help navigate potential landmines that may result from not being understood.

In building our new team from the ground up, I spend a lot of time doing drive-bys. I was new to a large and very complex organization, and I needed allies to help move the organization beyond the status-quo as well as to receive valuable feedback on how we could continue to improve our service delivery. "The Helpless Desk is of no help at all! Where do you get these people from! I don't know why I even bother to call!" During my drive-by interactions with nurse managers, administrators, physicians, and a slew of other not-so-well-meaning critics, these comments were unrelenting. That is the nature of service delivery—you get feedback. Most of the time, it's not so good. Sometimes an occasional "good job" will float your way. It's best to prepare for the former and not expect the latter. Those first eighteen months in our resurrection project were exciting and brutal. Some alliances came easy, while others required something that didn't come naturally to me: patience. I had come from an organization that was extremely large, but because of their plethora of resources, they maneuvered like a speedboat instead of a battleship. If it was broken, it got fixed quickly. Period.

This new organization didn't have the same level of commitment throughout its cultural core with respect to processes at that time. Longstanding traditions and cultural norms reigned supreme. In some pockets, as with many organizations, some norms will simply never be completely uprooted. It sometimes took a long minute to get things done. The first year or so was tremendously frustrating. I saw clearly a needed improvement stall right before my very eyes. There was a lot to do. I picked my battles, listened, and learned; I acted like I'd been there before and trusted the new relationships being built with the good eggs who also wanted better for the organization. I was flying blind, yet I'd never seen things more clearly—or at least, that was the story I had to consistently tell myself. The truth is that some really good people carried me and our team through much-needed improvements. Like I said, we don't get there by our own boot-straps.

One of the keys to leading people is to be inclusive in the team-building process. Depending on your professional level, you as the leader will have to determine how inclusive you are. Not everyone can have open access to you directly, but everyone should be able to experience your leadership. If not, you have a serious problem before you even start your leadership transfor-mation. If you as a leader are closed off without extending your skill and experience to others who may benefit from it, you are seriously crippling your ability to win. Modify your approach to be inclusive as needed and give yourself away to a cause greater than what you possess alone. Serve others. The correct alignment of people, processes, and technology will reveal itself organically. Unobstructed by our fierce desire to fix and control the narrative by serving others, we indirectly move obstacles without even rec-ognizing they exist in the first place.

As we began to sort out the herd into those willing to stay and help the service desk improve, and those moving on or being encouraged to move on to their next venture, I noticed the team really enjoyed "grilling" potential service desk analysts during the interview process, particularly when I chose to conduct a panel interview, which sometimes included up to four staff members. Most of the time, it was three or fewer. My main objective would be to set the tone, make the candidate feel comfortable, intro-duce myself, then get out of the way and let the team get into their questioning.

Having the team interview the potential candidates accomplished several things. First, it improved the interview skills of my team members. It also taught members new to panel interview techniques exactly what was happening to them during the process from the other side of the table. It leveraged collective input from the team and not just the manager. This approach also made a clear statement that said, "Your input here matters, and I will listen to you and value your opinion."

Getting out of the way as a leader is vital. Your opinion is important, but the overall opinion of the team is more important. You as the leader are ultimately responsible for the team's outcomes, and the buck stops with you. Some leaders interpret that as permission to tell others whom to hire and whom to fire—no, you really can't. If that were the case, then there would be no need for you to be in the leadership position in the first place. You'd be a babysitter, not a manager, with very little authority. What you can do as a leader of other leaders is make recommendations and give your advice with seasoned and thoughtful experience. One of the worst things a senior leader can do is tell another leader for whom their success or failures they are responsible is whom to hire and whom to dismiss. Why? Because what you've actually done is tell that leader, "I don't trust you, and I'm in control." I won't even begin to tell you the damage that's been done by people trying to micromanage personnel decisions that are better entrusted to the leadership team. At best, it makes you an insecure leader; at worst, it makes you a hypocrite. Please don't put that clown nose on. Trust your leaders. They really do know what they are doing. That's why you placed them in those leadership positions in the first place. That being said, it is your responsibility to recognize that if a key hiring decision has been made this is not working out you are well within your rights to hold that leader accountable for the results of that hiring decision. If your alarm goes off, you should listen to it and start having some crucial conversations. Hiding from it doesn't make it go away—it stifles momentum that could be used to make people and teams better.

It worked. Getting the team to buy into this new way of working and creating a paradigm-shifting culture began paying dividends. What started out as a very uncomfortable process for some (being asked to serve on the interview panel) eventually evolved into routine excitement when my employees hoped to be selected for the next round of candidate reviews. The team learned how to run a meeting, how to be concise with their note taking, how to ask probing behavioral questions to get at the heart of how a candidate may or may not fit into our environment, how to read body language, how to be an instigator or supporter. All these skills were given to me by caring leaders early in my professional career. I was paying attention at least some of the time but especially when no one thought I was even listening.

As I included more of the team in the interview process, what was once a "professional cemetery" where people brought their careers to die became a launching pad for new achievements. Over the next several years, with improvements in people, processes, and technology, we became a much better representative of our business, providing IT support to our physicians, nurses, and administrators to enable them to provide exceptional patient care, one relationship at a time. However, we still had miles to go before we slept.

They quickly realized my style of leadership was not a dictatorship. There were clear boundaries but never walls. There is a vast difference between the two. Many leaders *say*, "I have an open-door policy," but their behavior must consistently support their claim. If they don't follow through, then it's simply window-dressing from some dusty, old management books read years ago when "open-door policy" was first introduced into the management lexicon. Not worth a hill of beans. How can you have an open-door policy if your door is closed most of the time? I understand the importance of wanting to avoid interruption during an important meeting, a call, or quiet focus time. The question is, are you using that as an excuse because you're emotionally closed off? Or are you really so busy that those in your care have been conditioned to not bother you because you've consistently demonstrated that you are not available? Only you know that answer.

This new team became fiercely committed in their desire to do well. Each day, I became prouder and prouder of how they showed up for the demands of such a thankless job as a service desk IT professional. Clients rarely called to congratulate them for a job well done. Occasionally, hospital team members would take the time to send an encouraging email about their positive experience when contacting the service desk. We loved receiving those bricks of credibility. I loved receiving them for our team members. It was rocket fuel for them. Genuine recognition from me was good. Getting kudos from a customer meant more; it validated their hard work that most never saw but took for granted. Well-placed recognition pays for itself many times over its initial delivery.

Another tool in my arsenal is the art of the handwritten note. Thank you, Mr. D. Farinholt and Mr. J. Wright, for demonstrating the timeless art of gratitude. Most of us know exactly what needs to be said in our heads, but we don't take the next step and stop, sit down, and put pen to parchment. Note-writing is a worthy pursuit that I would highly recommended to those who have not experienced the internal pleasure of crafting a purposeful, well thought out, brief note of sincere gratitude to another human being. That, my current and future leaders, is time well-spent.

Our team consisted of people who wanted to be recognized for their contributions, just like anyone else. They were starved for acknowledgment of the obvious. People didn't respect what this group was doing and how critically important their roles were to the delicate reputation of IT. Leaders encourage. Most people will respond more favorably to recognition than they will to money. The temporary spike in productivity associated with money does not hold a candle to the sustained positive discretionary effort that will outlast the additional currency over the long term. You may be thinking about a time when this statement applied to you. Perhaps someone poured positivity into your life for a job well done that surpassed any financial platitude. You felt genuinely appreciated and valued. Money is good, and sometimes even great, but being truly respected for what you do and how you do it is awesome in a way that money just cannot buy.

The years would move quickly. Tick-tock, tick-tock. The comings and goings of quality people into our service desk family reinforced our belief that there was always another just waiting for us to discover them. Sometimes, this new discovery would be them discovering the service desk. Before long, the word was spreading throughout the organization that this team was actually a great place to work! Imagine that. The graveyard perception was now being replaced by internal candidates getting *excited* about the opportunity to come work in IT at the service desk. It was a good problem to have—people wanting to be a part of something new, purposeful, and exciting. It was a pleasant surprise for most of them; it was not what they were accustomed to. What was known in some sarcastic circles as the "helpless desk" became a place where people were actually clamoring to become a part of this new team on a completely new trajectory.

When the rubber meets the road and all hell breaks loose in the service desk, proudly watching my team perform under pressure filled my heart with joy. Nothing made me prouder than sitting and observing the team perform when chaos was infiltrating our camp due to something major going belly-up in the IT space regardless of the root cause—hardware, software, application, human error, or environmental event—not needing to get into the weeds with the team because I trusted their ability was refreshing. My trust was consistently rewarded with focused competency, effort, and professionalism to match. Managing events and directing personnel does not mean you have to do it all. Having quality people who can do most of it is a much better winning proposition. Your role as a leader is to develop strategies that require execution; your job is not always to *do*. Those are the tactics. You have good people for that. The training, poise, accountability, and collective discipline required from all parties won out in stressful times at the service desk. A leader sets the tone early in their administration—good or bad, right or wrong, strong or weak, lukewarm or frosty. The speaker does matter. Don't believe me? Ask those who are listening.

Keeping score also matters. Metrics and KPIs were foreign languages for this particular service desk. If I wasn't so embarrassed about discovering this, I would have been amazed. Teams need structure, procedures, standards—and a willingness to execute these things. We were heading in the right direction. The battleship was starting to turn ever so slightly. Team members would rally around each other whenever possible; of course, they did, because the team was made up of people they had recommended. No matter how brilliant or talented a person is, if they can't work with the team or the team is not on board with them, the chances of me hiring them were slim to none. I have on occasion made a couple of not-so-good hires. Guilty as charged. If you're fortunate enough to be in this management game long enough, you will invariably make a few bad hires. Remember, that's not the hard part. The part that determines team success or failure is what you do after making the mistake. For me, it was not a difficult decision—negatively impact one person or everyone? The choice was and continues to be simple: "Let's figure out how to get you into a role that better fits your personality and skill set. Thank you for your service."

Most of time, the casualty was self-imposed in order to avoid the inevitable. To my surprise, the team would get upset that they had allowed one to "get through the cracks" to me and waste our time. It was not time wasted. It was a lesson learned. There is always some good that can be extracted from the bad if we are willing to search for the truth in the lesson. They had also invested time in the candidates who didn't work out. They had their own skin in the game. Although over the years we didn't have many hiring failures, they were fully vested in the success of the service desk, and it manifested in their loyalty. It inspired me to see their positive discretionary effort grow with each passing day. If you want to see your team exponentially increase their discretionary effort, give them your unconditional loyalty—not your situational loyalty. If they choose to squander it, now you course correct. Don't be conveniently loyal when it suits you and your endeavors. That will not only decrease their commitment to you; it will also increase their resentment in your leadership. Disingenuity is a slow poison kills from within. You may not even realize this is happening to you because you're blinded by selfish ambition that squanders the leadership currency of respect and influence. Forgetting to serve others will quickly erode your success.

I'm a sucker for a great quote. Here's an excellent one that I discovered by way of a fortune cookie: "Business is like a tennis match: you typically win when you serve well."

I sometimes wondered if I was leading them or if they were leading me. That is what was nice about the journey: we simply wanted to win together, and we didn't care who got the glory. I made sure I would cover them from being placed in harm's way as much as possible.

Leaders cover.

Chapter Seventeen

Leadership Lesson Sixteen: Persevere.

If you believe in what you are doing and you are serving others, do not quit. As we unpack the nuances of this important character trait, it's important to understand the leadership context from which I am choosing to address this situation. The years 2013 through 2016 are what I call the "Valley of Despair years." These were the roughest, toughest, most frustrating years of my career. They were also the most developmental. This was an incredibly tumultuous time filled with professional incompetence and abuse of power, and on most days, this was all before nine a.m. This period in my professional life sucked. Having poor, uncaring leadership that is committed to only their own professional advancement at the exclusion of others is exhausting. Don't feel sorry for me; that's not my intent. I simply want to be honest about how tough a pill that period was for me to swallow. There was no support for me or the team, who were all completely and emotionally removed from our successes or failures. Our team's struggle to persevere against this narcissistic, Napoleonic behavior was only surpassed by this so-called leader's consistently morally bankrupt professionalism. This clown was a *gem*. Please accept my sarcasm here as an attempt to mask my heartbreak during this period that impacted so many others at the service desk who only sought to give their very best every single day. My heart ached for them and their pain as much as it did for my own turmoil.

I learned the value of sharpening my sword of perseverance. I learned how to fight through the frustration of knowing I was a committed team member seeking the good of the organization, and that spirit of professionalism and genuine respect was not reciprocated. I learned to suppress my feelings because it was made clear that my voice did not matter. I learned to stay true to what was immovable—my character and my service to others. Pouring myself into others through mentoring, professional development, personal and professional drive-bys to other colleagues seeking advice, or team building exercises to remind the team of how much they were valued became my saving grace.

The other rock during this period was my wife, Cynthia. As I've said before, she is a superhero masked as a loving spouse. Her encouragement and constant reminders of what was truly important—building a team and serving the organizational mission through technology—kept me not only sane but covered me with the full armor of her faith, her unconditional love that, although it went unseen by others, was real nonetheless. Sometimes being protected from our own internal "stinking thinking," which can cause us to make faulty decisions, is the best medicine. That is called grace and mercy.

A lot of people deal with their own poor leadership every day. The belief, whether perceived as true or not, creates a reality that you nor I are completely immune from. It just sucks when it's happening to you—the poor inaccurate performance evaluations; repeated character assassinations built on hyperbole and anecdotes along with documented misrepresentations parlayed into perceived truth that other so-called leaders accepted as accurate. Leading a team through this turmoil was such a beneficial growth period for me on a multitude of levels. Unbeknownst to me at the time, the team rallied around me. The service desk team and a few others close colleagues carried me. They saw my pain. They were familiar with the struggle because they were sometimes impacted as collateral damage. What made matters worse was that these mangled leadership moves were not covert operations. They were in my face, up close, and extremely personal. This was not business at all. Once again, I was being taught a lesson—"Stay in this box, and don't even think about trying to get out. *We* are in control of *your* career."

I wish I could tell you I was the only one being affected, and it was all about me. But this particular person was equally abusive to many others as well—including senior leaders. At least he was consistent. My burden of perseverance came in part because of my polite tenacity; I refused to just roll over and be one of his victims. His wake of destruction was enormous. People were devalued, their contributions not recognized, and their creativity minimized. He acted like the smartest guy in the room *all* the time. As you can imagine, the enormous chasm of negative discretionary effort grew larger every day under this cloud of narcissistic command and control.

There was, however, a sobering light at end of this long, dark tunnel. Perseverance builds character, and character strengthens into faith. If we simply endure and stay committed to what we know to be true, we will be victorious. The slightest glimmer of light at the end of that tunnel, which seemed so far away, grew brighter with each step forward. My wife once put it beautifully:

"Don't worry about it; he'll fall on his own sword, and you won't have to lift a finger." It was true. That's exactly what happened. She's so much smarter than I am. We just had to persevere, stay true to helping others, be transparent, work for something greater than ourselves, and believe that light would win over darkness. Our professional careers, as well as our journey through this life, may not play out when and how we expect it to. But good things will happen. We win. If you get nothing else from our brief time together, get this—we win. We are winners, and not losers. We are the head, not the tail. No weapon formed against us shall prosper. You have the choice to be and do the exceptional. It's already inside of you. Choose wisely. The world is waiting for you and your special gifts. Other people do not get to define your level of mediocrity or exceptional accomplishment. Your choices light the path you will walk, although not necessarily alone. It just sometimes may feel that way. Persevere.

Here's an additional takeaway, which requires some reflection. Be very careful about how you treat others when pursuing your selfish goals. Your goal may be as genuine and pure as the driven snow, but is it what you've been created to do? The temporary status and fortune that most people equate with success is a temporal illusion designed to keep you distracted from your true calling. Each day we wake up and make a conscious decision to choose to be happy, sad, apathic, excited, mediocre, good, excellent, or prolific. What you believe is what you believe and is directly proportional to your behavior as a person, not to mention as a leader. It has such a profound impact on your ultimate destination. I recommend giving your thought life some consistent care and feeding when appropriate. Introspection has been a good tool for me throughout this journey. Another good tool is having a few trusted friends and family to keep me within the guard rails of sanity.

I believe that my destiny is tied inextricably to my burden. I've learned through others' insight and wisdom how to properly identify my burden. Your burden is that which troubles you to your most inner core and does not disappear with time—it multiplies in intensity. It troubles you so much that you have no choice but to act on it. For some it happens quickly. For others it may take years to identify. I would fall into the latter category. My burden is helping others win so humanity is all the better for my contribution to our collective existence in such a fleeting moment that will quickly disappear. For this I am fiercely unapologetic. I was placed here to motivate, help, and develop others through use of my God-given talents, written and spoken words, and deeds of service. Success through service to others. This is my calling. This is my purpose. I now know exactly why I am here, and I must tell you that it is a wonderful revelation to experience. For this, I want the same for you.

This part right here is the gratitude portion of the program. By being exposed to a different perspective and a strengthened understanding of exactly what's happening around me and through me, I am convinced and persuaded that your "true calling," if you will, is wrapped in that which burdens you. I must confess that when I first heard this rationale it didn't register with me. That's where spending time with experienced and caring leaders who can help you discern your purpose-driven direction clearly helps us to see what is not naturally available through our own limited insight and internal biases.

It's dangerous for any leader to lean exclusively on their own understanding. A leader who listens and accepts the wise counsel of others not motivated by selfish ambition shines like a brilliant lighthouse clearly visible in the midst of a dense fog. The beacon is unmistakably clear. It is immovable. These leaders take on the additional power of those who are entrusted to them as additional energy sources that will sustain them when their power nears depletion. The guidance given to them in times of need is also renewable energy if they are humble enough to receive it. Good leaders listen. Great leaders discern the foolishness from the circumspect and then have the courage to act on it.

The question often came from out of nowhere. It would always be harmless and friendly. It would sometimes catch me by surprise because the location would feel incongruous with the inquiry. The ask is personal when wanting to understand how to tie a bow tie. The curious nature to solve something at the moment of inquiry that seems to be so elusive always put a smile on my face. The ask is innocent in its delivery yet fraught with anticipation of hopeful optimism that could never be ignored or dismissed—even if it was the tenth time someone asked the question in their own, very personal and friendly way.

"I wish I knew how to tie a bow tie. Is it hard?"

The four seconds of silence that followed that question was awkward at times because the question occasionally caught me off guard. It sometimes took me a quick second to process without making the person feel like I was intentionally ignoring their question. The opportunity to share how to actually tie the bow ties was always a fun exercise for me. I would tell them, "People think it's really difficult, but it's not. It's not hard at all. I could show you in two minutes." When the situation allowed me to demonstrate how to tie the knot, the look of amazement from the inquirer at the apparent simplicity was also fun for me. And there you would have it. That two minutes was sometimes in a hallway, office, elevator, or conference room after a meeting. The sheer elation of watching someone tie their first bow tie without any assistance was very cool. The pride was fun to see on their faces as they succeeded in doing something once thought impossible.

People have been wearing bow ties since the seventeenth century, when Croatian mercenaries wore them to hold together the opening in their shirts during the Thirty Years' War, so wearing a bow tie in and of itself isn't anything special. What I enjoyed were the stories behind where the bow ties came from. Every bow tie has a story, as do the people who wear them. Those journeys of discovery find themselves open to interpretation by those who are fortunate to hear them.

Some people caught on immediately, while others struggled with the exercise. For those who attempted the tie with my instruction but failed miserably, the journey continues. I applaud their tenacity and endurance. Their request for assistance has been relegated to the occasional drive-by if they are in the vicinity and would simply like to give it another try. This group is the most fun group of all—woefully clumsy but enthusiastically willing, and they don't take themselves too seriously. The best way I can describe their journey is to give you my bowling analogy. I enjoy bowling because I'm not good at it. I just do it because it's fun. That is the joy of it. There is no expectation of improvement. If I get a strike, that is awesome. If I roll a gutter ball, I say, "Oh, well." It's about the journey. The same applies to the folks who struggle to learn how to tie the bow tie but keep coming back to see how it's done. This casual, friendly dance builds a bridge from both sides that meets at the intersection of curiosity and purposeful discovery.

For those who are eventually successful in learning to tie the bow tie, I get a kick out of seeing them strut their stuff with newfound confidence brought on by a classic accessory not easily worn by everyone. The many colors, styles, and patterns give the recently initiated a plethora of choices when developing their own style. Finding your own style is just like finding your own voice as a leader: there is an element of trial and error to it. It doesn't just happen overnight. Great leaders were once good leaders, who at some point were new and not very good leaders.

Teaching other people how to tie a bow tie also helped create something very important—new relationships. It was my way of giving back something that was given to me by Mr. Magoo, that delightful, caring little man with a huge heart, slow walk, and a masterful sense of humor.

As leaders, we must strive each and every day to be better than the previous day. Mastering the bow tie is no different. Skillfully crafting a perfect bow tie, just like improving our leadership competency, requires committing to "tie the tie" a little bit better each day.

Chapter Eighteen

It hit me in my junior year of college. It came out of nowhere, and it never escaped me after that moment. I was in my off-campus townhome, studying for an upcoming final. It was late—really late—or should I say very early in the morning? My hazy glance located the clock on the wall. It was 3:50 a.m. I'd already been grinding for nearly six hours.

I remember a couple of things about that morning. It was freezing outside. It may have been four degrees or something awful like that, because I remember complaining that our apartment's thermostat said it was eighty degrees, but it sure didn't feel like eighty degrees inside. The Shenandoah Valley can be brutal during the winter months, and that morning, Harrisonburg, Virginia, was no exception.

The other thing was that I kept falling asleep. My head would suddenly droop into my lap or onto my book without warning. One minute I was awake—next minute asleep—one minute awake—next minute asleep. This dance went on throughout the night and well into the early morning. Right up until 3:59 a.m. What happened next, I cannot explain. Let's just call it a "unique discovery" that I didn't know about myself. Most of you have this within you, too, but some haven't figured it out yet.

Here's what I learned more than thirty years ago that I've carried with me to this very day. I accidentally discovered my "magic hour" was. It was 4 a.m. Over the next semester and all through my senior year, I solidified the discovery that I was the sharpest version of myself between the hours of 4 a.m. and 5 a.m. Long before the invention of 5-Hour Energy shots, there was No-Doze. Younger readers may not know about those, but my veteran readers are likely smiling. They know all too well. I discovered I didn't need those either.

So, there I was: sleepy as hell, and then all of a sudden, I wasn't. It was like someone flicked a switch and turned on every light in the apartment as the sun came rising brilliantly out of the east filling me with an abundance of strength and stamina. It took me some time to really buy in to this new reality, so I played with this new discovery for several weeks by purposely trying to fake myself out. I'd go to bed early one day, wake up a 2 a.m., go to be bed at 3:30 a.m. the next day, purposely sleep-deprive myself, then get up at 4 a.m. thinking I'd simply go back to sleep—but nope. I was wide awake and ready for anything. It was my hour. Everything seemed to slow down and become crystal clear. What were once blank pages were suddenly filled with words that actually made sense. What was vague became specific. What was vastly incomprehensible to me during this foggy period, I now understood. I had found my hour. My hour had found me.

Most of us never find our magic hour. For some, it's 1 p.m. Whatever the time is, after speaking with others who have discovered their "hour of power," I now know that this time period truly does exist. Now, I am not a scientist studying biorhythms, so that is not the point here. The point is everyone should pause and reflect on when they are their absolute sharpest; when they become the tip of their own spear, if you will. What time of day is it when everything just makes sense to you? When you feel your most powerful, energetic, and alive? Nothing can detract from your energy during this period. Everyone should find that magic place for themselves. At worst, you should know when you're not at your best. Most people can tell you that information. How curious is that?

Try locating your magic hour. You will be glad you did.

Rising and willing myself to move at 4 a.m. has become such a deeply ingrained ritual for me that sleeping late (any time after 6 a.m.) feels foreign and lazy to me. When your normal becomes their exceptional, that is when you exceed expectations. I also discovered that this was the best time for me to work out at the gym, which would be a safe haven throughout the seasons of my life. Physical activity has always been an important tool for my wellness. Take your medicine (self-care) now so you don't have to take all those other medications (big pharma) later. I'm asking everyone to be ridiculously selfish about this. No one on the planet will love you like you do or understand you better than you do. This journey of self-care should be taken with the same relentlessness mirrored in all of your other pursuits. We do what we enjoy. We spend time on things that are important to us. Basic human nature dictates this truth.

You might argue that you don't have time. The truth is, you don't have time to *not* invest in self-care—whatever "self-care" means to you. The human body is a spectacular creation. We only have one. Self-care is mandatory. Smart people—and smart leaders—understand how important good health is and make time for this beneficial pursuit. Others make excuses.

I am the epitome of an oxymoron. You see, I was the guy

who inhaled cigars and drank alcohol with the best of them, but I somehow found the energy to battle through that contradiction for years. I stressed my body and cared for it at the same time—for years. So, before I come at you saying, "Do better," I had to also become better. We are all works in progress, so no judgements here. "Decide, do, rinse, and repeat." I came up with that in the middle of a twelve-mile morning run—and I wanted to quit. Those four little words came to me in my fatigue and drove me to the finish. They have now become a signpost for times when all I have is the intrinsic motivation to guide me. Leaders figure out a way. Leaders decide, leaders do, they rinse and then they repeat.

I'm cigar-free now for almost eight years. During a time of intense personal struggle, I leaned heavily on the escape alcohol provided. I used it to hide the pain of that struggle, not as a casual enjoyment of life. Now behind me, the darkness has long since been replaced by the new adventures life has placed before my footsteps. I find myself cautiously on guard as to not to digress back to times that quite frankly are not a good look for me. Truthfully, at times even now, I have enjoyed an adult beverage or two. Now, I just don't beat myself up about it. I continue to be a work in progress filtered by the experiences that make me uniquely me.

The leadership lesson here is to have the accountability of others and their care to withstand those moments when casual embellishment wants to move to overindulgence. Ultimately, the responsibility is my own, and I do not abdicate my self-control to another. I own it. I walk in it. Suffice it to say it's good to have boundaries and those who hold you to them. I could not have successfully traveled this road alone. I needed help—like many of you who at some point may have battled or are battling some sort of addiction. The struggle is as real for me as it is for you. It is not the end of the journey but the beginning. I've said it before: asking for help is not a sign of weakness but strength personified. It is the warrior in us who humbles themselves to the realization of our fallible nature and seeks refuge in the help of others. The coward believes they can conquer their demons alone. Vulnerability is a necessary requirement for personal success. The proud rarely conquer their demons. Our mind is where the war all begins. It is the ultimate battlefield. The good news is that your battlefield will also have others willing to fight for and with you. Please, let them in so we all can triumph together. Real talk . . . they were sent by someone a lot smarter than both you and me. Sometimes we just don't recognize the essence of what's directly in front of us. We have all we will ever need if our hearts are first open to receiving it.

Leadership is about modeling the outcomes and the behaviors well before others join the party. Whether it's a brisk walk, training for your first 5K, or changing your diet, deciding to honor the one and only body you have is a smart decision. Leaders recognize there is an issue on the table and respond accordingly by developing a strategy, soliciting expert advice on topics specific to their needs, and then executing it consistently. Over time, the results of their focused dedications yield significant dividends and stabilize that leader to become even more effective at helping their organization deliver positive results.

Chapter Nineteen

A sharp dresser. A bit old-school. His clothing was just a tad big. He was energetic and enthusiastic. Those were my initial thoughts of Reuben S. I liked him immediately. As a thirty-plus-year veteran of the medical center and a student of IT, Reuben had cut his teeth initially in the clinical space, transitioned to IT, and is now a well-respected member of the senior leadership staff. Reuben knows his stuff.

As the manager for the service desk, my interactions with Reuben during our formative, early relationship were mostly healthy discussions on topics ranging from politics to fitness to clinical informatics to leadership biographies and more. Reuben loved to read and learn. I liked that about him. He continues to be an intrinsically motivated over-achiever who loves learning and has a passion for helping others. We would get along well over the years. The world of clinical information technology would place us in similar circles often, even though our IT areas of expertise were vastly different. At that time, I represented the service desk, the customer-facing portal for the organization, while Reuben was the director for the clinical applications teams responsible for the management of our electronic records. We would collaborate on projects, organizational deliverables, and departmental initiatives designed to improve our evolving culture as well as the entire medical center's direction. Our medical center has world-class researchers, physicians, teachers, and administrators who continue to garner recognition around the globe. Reuben, in my opinion, had a little something to do with that.

He and I each gave what the other needed without consciously trying. My direct approach was balanced by his more deliberate, less aggressive style. This made our relationship stronger without either of us diminishing the other. There were and still are times when we bounced ideas off each other, and after collaborating, we decided on the other person's recommendation. I appreciated Rueben's perspective just as much as he appreciated mine. Sometimes however, at the end of the day, you must go with what you know to be true to your heart. Even when we did not see things through the same lens, we both recognized each other's position. Respect does that. Envy, pettiness, and low self-esteem do not allow respect to flourish.

What is most interesting about our relationship to me was distance playing against closeness, which put us somewhere in the realm of a twilight zone brotherhood that I simply cannot put my finger on. I understand that this description may sound strange, but it is what it is. I'm grateful for our relationship. I thank God for it. I release the need to understand it. More importantly, I'm grateful to Reuben for helping me learn the operational complexities of an academic medical center. He introduced me to talented people who allowed me to help develop the service desk and work with professionals who have become allies who believed in the collective vision of this new service desk team and the direction in which we were headed.

Here's another funny thing. For years, I walked around

wearing nice clothes, thinking that "comfortable" was looking good on me. Here's another example of how my wife, Cynthia, is once again, so much smarter than I am. She helped me understand the difference between "comfortable" clothing and "fitted" clothing tailored and designed specifically for me. I used to see fitted tailored clothing as tight and uncomfortable, so I went the to the opposite end of the spectrum. What I thought was comfortable clothing was actually too big for me. I thought it was a decent look, and it was—except for the undeniable fact that the clothes were too big. I like that I can laugh at myself. It's really funny when you don't even know that you're being funny to others, and your true friends tell you later. Reuben and I both wore clothes that were a bit large for us. We have both made the proper course corrections while maintaining the love for the one constant that never goes out of style—the bow tie.

It's interesting, really, how you can think one thing about yourself while others see you completely in a different light. Most of the time, you simply don't get a chance to see that difference until something happens to bring it to the surface. That difference in viewpoint makes all of us unique. How we see the world can steer us in a direction that may often feel random. Sometimes those events that appear on the surface to be coincidental take you in exactly the right direction, even when that direction doesn't seem right at first. Being comfortable is oftentimes confused with progress. Leaders understand the difference between uncomfortable growth and change devoid of purpose and strategy.

Moving the service desk forward required making everyone

uncomfortable—even me. My personality does not naturally seek out help. My natural go-to is all about acceptance, decision-making, and consequences.

Accountability, another important leadership competency, requires a clear, concise plan of attack in order to become successful. It also requires a decision. You as the so-called leader must decide what type of team, department, or organization you're going to build. Make a decision and have the audacity to stick with it—even if it costs you politically, socially, or professionally. Your values should never be up for sale. What price, as the leader, are you willing to pay? As the late, great founder of Apple, Steve Jobs once said, "If you want to make everyone happy, don't be a leader. Sell ice cream."

As the team morphed into something new, improved, and much different from their former selves, I leveraged the experience of others as needed. You cannot move a team until you understand who you're planning with. Who are your rock stars? Who are your steadily performing worker bees? Who is your bottom ten percent? Every organization has these people. Manage or direct it. Otherwise, it will manage you, and then, my friend, it's too late. You will be planted firmly in the realm of the reactive leader, wondering why you're not seeing the results you expect. Great leaders ask, "How am I contributing to this issue?" Misplaced ambition can create a blind spot that we must be wary of. It will sneak up on you, and before you know it, you're missing the yellow caution flags because you're looking at your next promotion.

Let's not forget the second shoe that will most certainly drop due to your conscious decision not to act. By neglecting these potential gems in the rough, you not only miss an opportunity to mentor and potentially grow a key segment of your team, but you also allow the slow poison to remain in bloodstream. Remember the rock stars? Remember that positive discretionary effort we mentioned a hundred pages ago? Make no mistake about it: the longer you neglect your rock stars and decide not to address the bottom ten percent simultaneously, the more your discretionary effort from your rock stars will diminish. They will see issues that clearly need to be addressed go ignored, and if that becomes normal, they will lower their output. Why expend extra effort here when the slacker next to them won't even do the minimum and no one utters a word? As the leader, you are responsible for the development of every single member of your team, not just those you feel comfortable working with. Taking people for granted is far worse than taking technology or process for granted. Some technology just works—all the time. Some processes are tested and true. People, however, are not static deliverables. They morph into better or lesser versions of themselves as dictated by their intrinsic motivations, fears, successes, and environments, not to mention their leadership anchor which they look to when stability is both required and necessary.

There is absolutely nothing wrong with personal ambition if it's well-placed in service to something bigger than us. Ambition can also reward us on the journey to the professional relevance that some us seek. This genuine journey should be not only celebrated but cultivated. You experience the leaders who have connected the dots of mission and service with personal value. It's the other leader who wrangles the pretentious likes of others and false assurances into personal gain. Those who believe they can manipulate and control the future of those who rest within their immediate sphere of influence will invariably fail to generate the outcome they desire. We sometimes believe we have all the time in the world. We don't. We are a mist, here only for a fleeting moment in time. This is not a promise made, a promise kept. This is quid pro quo. Some call it playing politics; I'm sure there are many other names for this professional maneuvering. One such name that I give it is "white collar survivor," and it is such a colossal waste of time. It really is. Most can't see how much the game of politics wastes their time because of the successful trappings they have already secured. They already have the offices, titles, money, promotions, status, and leverage over others directly in their immediate sphere of influence, power, and control.

How does ambition manifest itself to the commoners? This term is not meant to be derogatory. I fall into this category. The term "worker bee" is used here to denote the layers of our socioeconomic status and position relative to others. Everyone wants to impose a label upon others that clarifies how they see the world. Everyone is a worker bee when they have to report to somebody in a higher position of authority. The fool's gold is when some leaders believe their status to be far superior to those in their immediate sphere. A fancy title doesn't make it so. It just makes it obvious. A fancy title says, "I'm in charge and you better know it!" A person with a fancy title uses position-power when threatened with skill and intellect from those they believe far less qualified than they.

Spend the time where it truly matters developing others

and lifting them higher. Accountability will help you do just that. Your title has more meaning when you don't ever need to use it because it has been surpassed by the respect and unconditional trust those in your care have already bestowed upon you.

Chapter Twenty

Over the last thirty years or so, I've probably helped fifty or a hundred people learn to tie the bow tie. I fondly remember the joy associated with each successful lesson. That same joy streamed across my face during that brief but successful lesson some thirty years ago in that small clothier with Mr. Magoo, my bow tie Jedi master.

Most leaders can recite their past failures quickly and with astounding precision. They can give you the date, time, and location their most epic miscalculations. "Uncanny" may be a good way to describe it. Nonetheless, it pains me to believe that far fewer leaders are more aware of their worthy successes. You see, we do a great job of remembering those things that work hard to hold us back. We are bound tightly to the failures of not only the recent but also of the woefully long ago.

Great leaders have short memories. As we rebuilt the service desk, there were failures. There were mistakes. We were trusting people we should not have been trusting. They were haters masked as supporters. We believed in the goodness of people over the misplaced ambition of power. We wanted folks to simply own their roles in situations that required two or more to tango, but not become an impediment to our success through disingenuous platitudes and left-handed compliments made only for the appearance of genuine concern. We truly worked for the good of the organization and the people within it. It was important that I instill in this new team the cultural shift in how we thought about what we supported every single day. This service desk team was and continues to be more than a password reset. This critically important team represents all of IT, whether you choose to believe that or not. Service is all of our responsibility. This is how we win. Real leaders embrace the totality of what they are responsible for. Leadership demands that we own it all—the good, the bad, and the ugly.

That team and a few trusted friends and leaders taught me the value of being a professional even when you want to be something totally different. Every once in a while, the angry little kid inside me would rear his head. Through the care and counseling of those who truly cared about my wellbeing (thank you, D. Kierson and Mike J.), I can see just a little more clearly what others have been aware of for years: Sometimes the best thing you can say is absolutely nothing. Let the clowns keep their clown noses firmly in place. You don't have to be the one to always take it from them when they've made it clear they don't want to hear from you anyway. It's the eyes. They give us away every time. They are the windows to the soul as well as the manifestation of what is in our hearts.

An important leadership note here: As a leader, it is vital that we understand the pulse of those we lead. Will we get it right all the time? Nope, but if we don't realize how critical it is that our teams be comfortable speaking freely, we will kill organizational momentum and completely undermine trust. When people choose to stop contributing, your leadership antenna should be asking some questions. There is something going on that requires a conversation. Ignoring it will not make it go away. This is where being direct will yield success. The success is not only in the outcome of the conversation; it is in the courage to have the conversation in the first place.

Leadership Lesson Seventeen: No good deed goes unpunished.

No matter the intent of the deed undertaken, someone is going to be a critic of it. You can simply count on it. Leadership requires you to be able to handle criticism, both constructive as well as the utterly useless. Remember, everyone has an opinion about *how* you should be doing everything. Keep it moving. Trust your instincts, experience, and intellect. Honor your journey and the commitment you have made to it. Removal of the personal affiliation we may want to attach to the feedback should be weighed carefully against the motives of the source. Any leader worth their weight can describe multiple times when they knew in their gut a particular decision should be made, and for whatever reason, they went in a completely different direction in order to appease the masses, not holding true to their conviction, and the result was an outcome that failed miserably, all because they wanted to make everyone else happy instead of doing the necessary, courageous thing. "Hello, it's Steve, how many flavors of ice did you say you're going to sell?" Here's where truly phenomenal leaders rise to the top. When the expectations of those in your care are so fundamentally distant from your own that you chose not to compromise your core value system—this is the moment you win, even if you temporarily, and in some cases permanently, lose the support of those who don't understand or care about your position. That good deed may appear to not be the right decision, but rest assured you may not find that out in the current moment. It may manifest itself elsewhere days, weeks, or years later. What may appear to be a very ordinary, singular decision may turn out to be a life-changing event for someone else. It may remain hidden from your periphery. It may not ever lend itself to your view. It may be for another person or moment entirely. What's difficult for most of us is understanding the complexities of the simple. We just overthink it. We simply want to know everything right now. It's reality that weighs into your mental gymnastics to remind you that you can't.

Watching Reuben tie his first bow tie unassisted made me so very proud. I was and remain genuinely delighted for him in mastering something he once thought difficult—with practice. But that is the answer to everything, I suppose: time, practice, and patience to endure the struggles of learning something new. Every time I see him floating as if on a magical carpet down the hallway, all decked out in his colorful bow tie and matching handkerchief ensemble, I smile with my Mr. Miagi joy. What's more impressive was watching the natural maturation of Reuben's bow tie skills develop as the months went by. What started as a good but clumsy effort blossomed into a beautiful bouquet of accessories that proved worthy of any well-dressed wannabe bow tie aficionado. Yes, Mr. Reuben had come a long way. His bow tie style was now his own. My work here was done. This was a very good deed, and I enjoyed the giving associated with it.

One of the most influential presentations I've ever heard came from a man I do not know and have never met but that has inspired and influenced me far above what my meager human capacity can comprehend. Pastor J.K. Jenkins, Sr., I thank you! His instruction on how to properly interpret the multitude of voices that we as mere mortals in addition to being leaders hear on a daily basis clearly placed leadership responsibilities in the proper perspective for me. His passionate and sometimes humorous delivery inspires and feeds my soul daily to such a degree that I now believe not only in the power of universe but also in the profound excellence of the human spirit. I am profoundly grateful to Pastor Jenkins for his daily scripture-filled inspiration. Pastor Jenkins, this work proves that what you do every single day matters. Thank you! Additionally, I'd also like to thank the following men of God who have also had a profound impact on my life; the Reverend Dr. Victor Davis; the Reverend Dr. Raymond Bell; the Reverend Dr. William Curtis and last but certainly not least, the Reverend Dr. Howard J. Wesley. Each of you in your own special way have utilized your call by the Holy Spirit to make a positive difference in my life as a true believer and completely redeemed sinner. The champion in all of us says, "Listen, this is going to be the way I work through you, not only for you, but for the benefit of the others who will be impacted by you. My life, as well as the lives of others with whom I share your messages with daily for the last several years, have been profoundly and positively impacted by each of you. I am unapologetic in my love for each of you and wish you nothing but success as you continue your walk in the best place of all, the perfect will of God.

It may not make sense at times. Trust and follow your instincts and stay committed to the path that you have chosen. There is a reason that a visceral energy burns within you. It is your purpose calling you. It's knocking on your door, and it will not leave—it will only wait for you to answer. The question is: Will it wait forever?

What I share next with you is what I believe to be true in my heart. The voice of my consciousness spoke to me with a calmness and clarity of purpose that exceeded my rationale. Unbeknownst to me, I had been cleaned up physically over the last several years in preparation for what would unfold years later. Remember, I still had to choose to listen and then act on what was being placed in my heart.

It is my belief that I was cleaned up, propped up, and positioned to be exactly where I was for something far greater than I could ever imagine. Through all of the newness of starting over, through the Valley of Despair years when I tried everything short of resigning, through the shade of other's people's foggy lenses and character misrepresentations, through the joy of watching so many quality people grow into better versions of themselves—I was still here. This place. This time. This moment. I am persuaded and convinced that the reason I was still in that service desk management position was because I was needed by someone else years before I even knew it. The universe knew what was happening even when I had no clue why I was putting down those things that were detrimental to my health. It is my belief that genuinely caring for others pulls you into a direction that may seem unfamiliar. No one can convince me differently. The power to reflect on all the preparation before the living donor event blows me away even when I think about it now.

I was fortunate to be chosen as a living donor. An honor that I reflect on every single day. Even as of this writing I do not believe that I fully comprehend the magnitude of the moment nor the decision. For my psyche that is a good thing. Don't overthink it. Just strive to be a good person. Just do your best to make a difference for someone else. Decide, do, rinse, and repeat.

Reuben and I now share something far more valuable than a penchant for silk bow ties. We share life. I am humbled to have been chosen. I am grateful to have been matched. But I am more impressed by the ridiculous timing and sense of humor in it all—an avid cigar smoker and more-than-occasional drinker was now propped up and medically cleared to give a kidney! Wow. I am convinced that situations have a way of working themselves out if we keep moving forward. Leaders don't quit. Leaders trust their instincts and the information at their disposal to make good decisions. Being able to understand and act on those instincts convicted me in a most profound way. It was simply the right thing to do and the right moment in which to do it. No questions. Trust, obey, and follow the path of continued service to others and causes that are bigger than you.

As a leader, you will enter that place where you just know that you know that you know. Trust it. Lean not to your own understanding. Don't get it twisted. The so-called leaders that think they know it all eventually lose their way if they are tripped up by the "look at how great I am" trickster lurking just beneath the surface of you often-times good intentions. To what you don't understand, ask clarifying questions. Gain as much clarity as your comfort allows, and then for that which remains, surrender. The answer may not be far away. Or it could be years in the making, and this moment is an important milestone in your eventual understanding. Listen with your head, understand with your heart, and watch the goodness of your actions show you how truly powerful of a person that may just happen to also be a leader you already are.

Remember, it's not all about you anyway.

December 2013 was even more pivotal than my kidney transplant living donor experience. Why? Well, if it hadn't been for others understanding the medical conundrum I was in at the time, I may not have been around to be of service to Mr. Reuben. I'm not a doctor, and I don't play one on TV, so I didn't understand the significance of my white blood cell count being over fifty thousand. Now I do. That's a bad white blood cell count—very bad. Let's call it what it was: potentially lethal. I had no idea what sepsis was either. Ignorance is bliss, but in this case, it could have been deadly.

My appendix was about to rupture, and I had no idea. I learned later that if that had happened to me, the toxins that my appendix was supposed to dispose of properly would permeate my bloodstream, causing sepsis, which if left untreated, would have resulted in multiple organ failure and possibly my demise. Here's another example of why my wife continues to be vastly smarter than me. She rushed me to the best level one trauma center in the country (VCU Medical Center), where they performed an emergency laparoscopic appendectomy. I'm sad to say that I was the epitome of the typical man—bravado all the way! "I'll be fine. It'll pass." I was very stupid when it came to my health on this day. Sometimes just throwing some dirt on it or just toughing it out isn't the best medical choice available.

One of the most important reasons I enjoy working at the medical center is the collective brilliance of the staff. Whether a nurse manager, nurse practitioner, surgeon, administrative professional, food service worker, or housekeeping team member, *everyone* matters. They make their jobs look easy every single day. As a level one trauma center, our team gets the best of the worst of things daily. When I tell you that I routinely get up from my office and walk to the hospital just to watch the clinical awesomeness that goes on every single minute throughout every single day, I mean it. Others call it rounding, visiting different hospital departments to better understand how they are run and how IT can improve their ability to provide exceptional patient care. I've done a lot of rounding. I continue to do rounding, especially unannounced. Some areas you can get away with that; other, more restricted locations require supervised escort. It's an ongoing education that I continue to be both astonished by and grateful for. That's the unselfishness associated with building relationships with business partners and medical staff. Finding out from the customer's perspective how we (IT) can be and do better. The lens of gratitude through which I view this organization far exceeds any businesslike activity. It is awe, appreciation, and respect that drives a passion in me to be better that I will not apologize for.

Think about this for a second. Someone with aspirations of serving others through their mastery of medicine will study thousands of pages of medical jargon and pictures in medical books that they must not only memorize but also comprehend—and then they must go on to display that technical knowledge with proficiency and caring skill to heal others. Keep in mind that, unlike with other incredibly fulfilling occupations, failing at this exam means people may die. Lives are at risk. Decisions are made in real-time that potentially impact families for generations to come. Years of study, sacrifice, and practice go into this. Yeah, we are talking about practice! Skill is acquired through the repetition of practice. Professionals make skill look routine. I am awestruck by how exceptional these clinical heroes perform every single day. I have no other word for it. They inspire me more than they will ever know. Their professionalism, competence, tenacity, and courage—not to mention intellect—keeps me grounded. I have zero desire to be the smartest guy in the room. We have plenty of other clowns for that. So, before you get too full of yourself and all of your accomplishments, just remember this: there's more air in that bag of chips than you think. Be and remain humble. A lot was done way before you got here.

And every so often, take a step back, appreciate the goodness and grace of others directly in front of you, and then remind yourself that it's never been about you anyway.

Conclusion

Most leaders evolve through mounds of experience, trial, and error. Aside from the years of study practicing a particular discipline, they commit to what fills them with purpose and passion. The years acquiring the technical knowledge are simply a placeholder to be used as the experience of the position shapes you into the leader you will eventually become.

Working hard is a foundational character trait. Most great leaders put in the requisite work to become that way. Great. Mediocrity requires zero skill. Simply show up. Don't do anything at all—keep quiet, don't ruffle any feathers, and there you have it. Congratulations: you are an average leader. Amazingly, some people will even find a way to call you excellent! I love this country.

That brings me to the point: people have their own subjective belief systems regarding what true, thoughtful, purposeful leadership looks like. We may each view the same person, group, or team quite differently, so it begs the question: What key attributes are undeniable in most great leaders? This list could be quite extensive, so let's not dilly-dally. Let's get to where the rubber meets the road. We may agree to disagree on my list, and that is okay. In fact, I would hope your list would be different from mine but share some quality adjectives on which we agree.

In my opinion, great leaders possess the following qualities:

- Inspirational
- Creative
- Delegative
- Accountable
- Authentic
- Compassionate
- Decisive
- Skilled Storyteller
- Business-minded
- Direct
- Durable
- Curious
- Value-driven
- Giver
- Life-long learner
- Humble
- Ambitious
- Servant-minded

Again, there are probably many characteristics not mentioned here that could be added to this list. This is just my list. I'd like for you to create your list and ask yourself the tough questions about why each quality made your list. This listing here represents my journey. I look forward to you sharing with me how your journey has helped others flourish, how your gifts are being unleashed for the world to experience. In the beginning of this book, we talked about this being not only an opportunity for me to share my story with you, but an opportunity for you to apply this content to your journey and see what becomes of your dreams. It is my sincere hope that you are inspired to move forward.

The impetus for my writing these words did not originate from me. The words came from deep within my soul, an intractable weight that I could not remove until I decided to act upon it. The agitation that accompanies the burning desire to act on what you can feel calls you from a place you cannot explain, but you understand that it is real and must be dealt with. The decision to not act only makes the agitation worse. You must move forward. You must not wait. You must not overthink it. You must take action. Others are waiting. The burden to share some of the many leadership lessons learned over the years was the driver that was placed within me to deliver content for the benefit of someone else. The unexpected will grab you by your collar and pull you where you don't really want to go. As a leader, you are already equipped with the foundational characteristics that have positioned you to be chosen to lead and care for others in the first place. You are supposed to be here. This is your time. I believe in you as a leader and power that is within you.

Your burden is calling. Can you hear it? Listen with your heart and not your head. Yes, I believe you can hear it calling you closer as clear as day. Here's a nugget that was given to me that I now give to you: Fear is not from God. Fear is the trick of the enemy to distract and discourage you. We have not been given a spirit of fear, but rather a spirit of love and power and a sound mind. You don't have to wish you tried something. Decide, and then go do that which you were called to do. You may stumble and even fall down. Get up. Try again. Never quit.

Rinse. Repeat. Truly inspiring leadership is courage wrapped in conviction, service to others, and enduring perseverance to see your dreams become reality.

That is how you win. That is how we all win.

Success Through Service

Soli Deo Gloria

Acknowledgments

This book would not have become a reality without continuous "nudging" from my Lord and Savior, Jesus Christ. He is my number one. Father, I thank you.

To my lovely and beautiful wife, Cynthia: I thank God for you. I am grateful for your love, patience, and encouragement throughout this journey of discovery. *I love you more today than all of my yesterdays.*

To our children, Jasmine, Sydney, Gabby, and Darius: we cover you daily with our prayers that all you achieve in this world becomes magnified in service to others through the power of the gifts and talents already inside you, placed there by the God the Father. This story would not have been written without you. I love you.

To Bernie and Dorothy Mann (along with Jodie, Sue, and Steve): thank you for taking in a kid from the sometimes-not-so-kind streets of Richmond, Virginia, and giving him another place to experience unconditional love. Thank you, Steve, for teaching me how to drive a stick-shift (that ugly brown Pinto) and getting stuck on the hill two blocks off Broad Street in rush hour traffic with cars everywhere! Most of all, thank you for showing me a world of people who didn't look like me that I still had very much in common with growing up. Thank you for showing me that I belonged.

To my Aunt Alice and my Uncle Russell: I am who I am

because you and the entire Brown clan took the responsibility of raising me when my natural parents were no longer available. Thank you for your love and unwavering support during my formative years. Thank you for being at my basketball games and graduations and saving newspaper clippings for my children to see many years later. Thank you for being the large stone that never moved. Thank you for keeping Christ in my life even when I didn't keep Him in mine. My love for you is forever! I am eternally grateful to have you in my life. Thank you. I love you more than you will ever know.

To Mr. Larry Rose: thank you. Thank you for allowing me to continue doing something that I truly loved doing at a time when others and their misplaced ambition didn't appreciate my love and service to a game that continues to bless me and my family to this very day. Thank you for being a true leader of men who chose the path less traveled of continuous basketball officiating instruction, training, discipline, accountability, and respect when others chose political expediency and the love for fame and fortune when your bedrock requirements of professionalism and loyalty remain unchanged. Thank you for not mincing words when clarity and conviction were all that was required. Thank you for simply being a true basketball mentor, colleague, supervisor, and friend. The assignments to referee basketball games will come and go, but my loyalty and respect to what you represent to me in my life and the benefit to my family will last forever. Thank you, sir.

To every basketball official I have ever worked with through the years, I say thank you for helping me learn a game I truly love and a craft that has blessed my life so abundantly. I have learned from you, mimicked a skillful basketball officiating mechanic from you (Leslie J.), learned how to deal with coaches (Dwayne G.), internalized the rhythm of the basketball game (Rose, Edsall, Brown, and Ward), and understood when to be a listener instead of an enforcer. Thank you for showing me the value of your experience developed many years before I even set foot on a basketball court. Thank you for your kindness and willingness to be a teacher, partner, and, in some cases, a real friend (Ayers, Eades, Kersey, Luckie, Cox, Crawford, Armstrong, Sanders, Bordeaux, Rivers, and Robinson). To every official who referees a child's game, please strive to be the official who, when others see your name on the schedule, they say, "Oh, yeah, good people are on this crew tonight!" Don't be the guy nobody wants to work with. Remember, officials talk. Never forget that your success had more to do with the others who helped you succeed than your own individual talent. We don't win this race alone. Be well regarded long after you leave the game. Every official has a finite number of games in their wheels (legs). Try not to overstay your welcome.

To my fellow officials starting anew, as well those moving through the ranks into the stratosphere of the refereeing elite: I will continue to cheer for your success in this child's game that we get to participate in for only a fleeting moment. Life is short. Continue helping other officials win, and watch your career be filled with something far greater than financial accolades, tournament appearances, or finals championships—the currencies of gratitude, respect, and influence that will never depreciate. Whether parochial league six-year-old Energizer bunnies (which are still my favorite age to referee to this day), AAU, recreational league or division I, II, or III—just remember this refereeing truism I recite that veteran officials gave me a long time ago: "You're not as good you think you are, and you're not as bad as they say you are. The fans are here to see the players, not you. Stay out of the way, be a good partner, cover your primary, and don't have the crew wind up on ESPN because of some boneheaded play that you screwed up!"

To my friends, colleagues, and acquaintances: allow me to simply say thank you for your presence in my life and the seasons in which you came. Some have remained to this very day, while others have transitioned into their next chapters. To Dan, Valerie, Larry, and Keith: thank you for keeping me off the ledge and for tying the rope around my waist that I couldn't see when I was either pushed or made the bad decision to jump into the lions' den. Your listening ear and counsel have proven invaluable my journey, which still continues to this very day. To all: I say that through every experience we traveled together, the reason for our coming together may not have been clear at the time, but just know that I value the lessons taught, words spoken, situations encountered, battles lost, and battles won. Thank you for being in my life. Our journeys together are integrally woven within the pages of this story. They are easily recognizable. I love you and value your continued friendship and support. Thank you.

Additionally, to my cousin, my "I'm always in charge" big sister, Denise: thank you for everything you've done over the years. When I couldn't be there, you were taking care of one of the most influential people in our lives—our Granny, Cornelia Payne. Thank you for your resilience. Thank you for your love.

To Granny: thank you for the many lessons you imparted

deep within my soul. Thank you for helping me understand that making the bed really had nothing to do with making the bed. Thank you for your wisdom, love, and ability to help me understand what hard work, dedication, and sacrifice looked like. Thank you for all those Sunday trips to see my father, even when I didn't understand the significance of the journey. Rest in peace, Granny. Edward loves you.

One last thing: thank you to those I've yet to meet. It is my prayer that some small piece of this book finds its way into your heart at its intended moment designed specifically for your success. The burden I feel to share some of my story may inspire others like you to not only dream but do. All things are possible to those who love Him and are called according to His purpose.

I hope you enjoyed this book as much as I enjoyed writing it. May God bless you and keep you safe.

—Harold E. Harris Jr.

About the Author

As a native of Richmond, Virginia, living kidney donor and graduate of Benedictine College Preparatory ('84) Harold E. Harris Jr. is an IT executive servant-leader with thirty-two years of progressive leadership experience in multiple technical disciplines specializing in service delivery and end-user computing management. Harold received his bachelor's degree in public administration and political science from James Madison University in 1988 and his master's degree in information systems and IT management from Virginia Commonwealth University in 2010. Most recently, Harold is certified as a Prosci Change Management Practitioner (CCMP) and a Six Sigma Green Belt. Harold is also an ITIL certified professional.

Beginning in 1989, Harold has cultivated a diverse background that includes fiscal management, clinical support management, telephony, networking infrastructure, desktop support, and hardware and software application support. In his current End-User Computing executive leadership role he is responsible for six intricate but vastly different teams (videoconferencing/telemedicine; virtual desktop infrastructure; SCCM/Active Directory application deployment; mobility services; collaboration services through Microsoft's Office 365 platform; SharePoint support) which is focused on delivering business value via servant leadership and sound technology management principles that the improve the customer's experience.

Harold continues to devote much of his time to mentoring young professionals, motivational speaking engagements, and giving back to the community. He currently serves on the board of directors for the not-for-profit organization VA Voice (located in Richmond, Virginia) which helps vision and hearing-impaired citizens of diverse backgrounds enjoy all the world has to offer through broadcasted programming that reads and performs content for those unable to see or hear it. Harold also has a lifetime relationship with the Omega Psi Phi Fraternity, Inc. His professional affiliations include SHRM, Prosci Change Management Practitioner, HIMSS, and ACHE. Harold is also an avid fitness enthusiast and intermediate yoga practitioner. For the last thirty-two years, Harold has served as an NCAA Division I basketball official.

A father of three daughters—Jasmine, Sydney, Gabrielle—

and one son, Darius—Harold currently resides in Stafford, Virginia with his ridiculously beautiful wife, Cynthia. They enjoy cruising to exotic locations, outdoor activities, and spending quality time with close friends and family.

Please connect with us by joining our email distribution for notifications of future publications at www.frombasketballto-bowties.com. For speaking engagements, please connect through our social media platforms listed below.

EMAIL ADDRESS: Service@SourceOneConsult.com
TWITTER HANDLE: @SourceOneRVA
INSTAGRAM HANDLE: SourceOneLLC
WEBSITE: https:\\www.SourceOneConsult.com